The
PROPHETIC
PROMISE
of the
SEVENTH
DAY

BOOKS BY BRUCE D. ALLEN

Promise of the Third Day

AVAILABLE FROM DESTINY IMAGE PUBLISHERS

The Fulfillment of Every Covenant Promise

The
PROPHETIC
PROMISE
of the
SEVENTH
DAY

BRUCE D. ALLEN

DESTINY IMAGE® PUBLISHERS, INC.

P.O. Box 310, Shippensburg, PA 17257-0310

"Speaking to the Purposes of God for This Generation and for the Generations to Come."

This book and all other Destiny Image, Revival Press, MercyPlace, Fresh Bread, Destiny Image Fiction, and Treasure House books are available at Christian bookstores and distributors worldwide.

For a U.S. bookstore nearest you, call 1-800-722-6774.
For more information on foreign distributors, call 717-532-3040.
Or reach us on the Internet: www.destinyimage.com.

ISBN 10: 0-7684-3159-X
ISBN 13: 978-0-7684-3159-9

For Worldwide Distribution, Printed in the U.S.A.
1 2 3 4 5 6 7 8 9 10 11 / 14 13 12 11 10

Dedication

This work is dedicated to my amazing wife, Reshma. Your love, encouragement, confidence, and support have been one of the greatest treasures this life has to offer. I could not have written this without you. You are the love of my life, my greatest earthly friend, and my heart. I treasure each and every day we have together, and I treasure you.

Acknowledgments

To my best friend, my healer, my Lord, and my soon-coming King, Jesus Christ, who redeemed me and called me by name.

To my parents, Ed and Shirley Allen, who have always encouraged me. Thank you.

To my pastors Barry and Kay Hill, who made room for us to share this word.

To Jerry and Chip Foster, true forever friends.

To pastors Bruce and Sherri Gunkle, whose ministry inspired and set me free.

To our intercessors, especially Neil Lowery, whose prayers cover us and keep us in His care.

To Faye Higbee, who helped to edit this book and make it possible. Thank you.

To the many who have asked for another book—here it is!

Endorsements

What does it mean for us as believers that we are now living in The Seventh Day? What promises should we expect? My friend Bruce Allen will open your eyes and heart to the answers to these questions as he passionately presents his in-depth study *The Prophetic Promise of the Seventh Day*. Last year, our Church was blessed as Bruce taught us these promises. Now you will be blessed as you read!

Pastor Barry A. Hill
Christian Life Church
Spokane, Washington

I would urge anyone who wants to know God's plan and purpose for life today to read this book. People are facing many challenges and situations today that can drain the love, joy, and peace from their souls.

Through *Prophetic Promise of the Seventh Day*, you will be empowered to face your challenges and live life to the fullest through the revelations revealed from God's Word for you in this book. You will find it contains biblical directions for such a time as this.

T. Edward Allen
Pastor/Evangelist
Storehouse Ministries International
Spokane, Washington

Many things are being written these days concerning the supernatural. I believe this is God provoking faith in His Church according to what will be needed to get the job done in what has quickly become perilous times. This book fits that same bill with something more. There is absolutely no compromise with the necessity of godly character. Bruce Allen calls to us from the pages of his work on two fronts. The first, to a new realm of faith for once again biblical exploits. The second, a Christ-likeness that bears little or no resemblance to much of what we see being offered today. These two essentials are needed for global transformation and are a recurring theme throughout this work. This book is not for those satisfied with the status quo but rather those who are in pursuit of God's present truth making the difference now.

Glenn Dunlop
Senior Pastor
Highway of Holiness Church
Belfast, Northern Ireland

I have known Bruce Allen for the past five years and have participated in his meetings here in Malaysia. When Bruce takes centre stage, *be still and know that God is present*. He has his finger on the pulse of God's direction on every occasion of his ministry.

This awesome book contains revelations of Scriptures connecting to actual current events which are succinct and written with accurate key ingredients because it is so evident that Bruce hears from the Lord. Called to be a prophet to the nations, his teachings are so immersed deeply in revelation and understanding of the Word.

I heartily recommend this book, as it contains the same anointing, fervency, and depth which Prophet Bruce carries when he ministers. This book has been written in the right season of the Lord and will undoubtedly raise the Body of Christ to the next level of preparation for the second coming of our Beloved Lord Jesus.

This book is a must for the Body of Christ. Be blessed.

Rev. Dr. Collin Gordon
Senior Pastor
Trinity Community Centre, Malaysia

Herein is Bruce Allen at his best. His prophetic insights chronicle and effectively trumpet where the Church is and where it's going. It contains relevant, simply stated, and much-needed clarification of a mystery for most Christians—the seventh day! It breaks through the veil of types and shadows, bringing down to earth heavenly understanding of the times and seasons. The Sabbath rest, the Enoch generation, the fulfillment of every covenant promise may literally be at our doorstep, and we need to be alert to what He is saying and doing right now! Well written and easily understood—this is a must-read.

Pastor Bruce Gunkle
City of Refuge
San Antonio, Texas

Bruce Allen writes with clarity as a leader with a global perspective. His insights are fresh and challenging. You may not agree with all of the author's conclusions, but the reader must acknowledge that Dr. Allen has researched well and writes from a deep devotion to our Lord. This book calls for a serious read. You will be enriched by the Kingdom principles articulated in this text.

Rev. Dr. John Roddam
Rector: St. Luke's
Seattle, Washington

As I sit in my office on the eve of Pentecost Sunday, May 31, 2009, my heart reflects on the movement of the Spirit of God upon the Church in Acts and the amazing joy that came to entire cities because an obedient people moved out in the fire of that hour. There was a power to release people from sickness, to raise the dead, to cleanse those with incurable diseases, and to have authority over demonic influence. When Jesus left this earth, He left us with the "baby stuff." The Holy Spirit came and endued with power those who were hungry for more. He also said, "Greater works will you do" (see John 14:12).

We are moving into the finest hour the Church has ever known! There's a fresh hunger that has come to a "Joshua Generation" who lingers in the "meeting tent" for more…to be endued with the power to release the greater things. Acts 17:28 says, *"for in Him we live and move and have our being, as also some of your own poets have said, 'For we are also His offspring.'"* The book, *The Prophetic Promise of the Seventh Day*, by my good friend Bruce Allen, is a must-read for those who desire to move as "His Offspring."

My wife Ruth and I highly endorse this book for the equipping of this Seventh-Day generation, who are finding their identity in Him and are being positioned in God's Kingdom for global harvest.

John Filler
Ministry Overseer
The Gateway Ministry Resource Center
Coeur d'Alene, Idaho

"It is not for you to know the day and the hour when I will come back again," the Lord Jesus told His disciples. Bruce Allen in this book has convincingly argued that we are living in the seventh day which is the last hour. The events of the world point to the soon coming of Jesus Christ. The Church, as the Bride of Christ, must get ready. As Bruce clearly demonstrated in this book regarding the return of Jesus Christ, we are living in the Seventh Day. The truths expounded upon in this book are given by the Lord to His servant by revelation knowledge. We should heed the warning, and like the five virgins, we must correctly discern the times and get ready for the coming of the Bridegroom. Bruce Allen has made a significant contribution to the Body of Christ.

Cannon James Wong
Father of the Charismatic Renewal in Southeast Asia

Contents

Foreword

Across the globe, God's people have been crying out for a greater understanding of the strange times in which we live. Witnessing the deterioration of moral society and the often disturbing events unfolding throughout the world, some are gripped with fear, and others wonder if God has forgotten them. But God hasn't forgotten! He's very much at the center of it all, and everything is right on schedule. This is no time to fear, but a time to rejoice as we have entered into a wondrous slice of God's divine timetable: *The Seventh Day*.

I'm fully persuaded that one avenue in which God has answered His people's plea to better understand the current age is through Dr. Bruce Allen, who has spent countless hours in God's presence to study, pray, and listen to God's voice regarding the spiritual and prophetic significance of this season. Part of the revelation Dr. Bruce received from God regarding the key time in which we live, was shared in his previous book *The Promise of the Third Day* (Destiny Image). If you haven't already, I highly recommend that you also read *The Promise of the Third Day*, as it lays a solid foundation for what you're about to receive. These two anointed works go hand in hand to complete an amazing prophetic picture of God's plan before He closes the curtain at the end of this age.

I've had the privilege and honor of knowing Dr. Allen for many years. When I first met Dr. Bruce, I thought of Peter and John, who had been called on the Sanhedrin carpet after healing the crippled man at the Gate Beautiful. The Bible says that after Peter, filled with the Holy Spirit, explained that the mighty name of Jesus Christ had healed the man, the council *"took note that these men had been with Jesus"* (Acts 4:13 NIV). Likewise, it seemed obvious to me that Dr. Bruce had been with Jesus. In fact, it's been obvious every time we've crossed paths that Dr. Allen walks with Jesus daily.

I believe *The Prophetic Promise of the Seventh Day* is a result of the time Dr. Allen has spent in the Lord's presence. The timely, yet critical message God has deposited in Dr. Bruce is a gift to the Body of Christ. Thank God for the opportunity we have been given to partake of the fruit of the labor sown into this anointed work. I believe it will further equip God's people to stand strong to the end.

Fueled with a passion for God and the revelation with which God has entrusted him, Dr. Allen will not only enlighten you to God's promised blessings for the Seventh Day, but will teach you how to position yourself to walk in those blessings to the fullest. Offering a sound message that exposes the challenges Christians will face as this age comes to a close, *The Prophetic Promise of the Seventh Day* shares scriptural wisdom that will better equip you to fulfill God's divine destiny. As Dr. Bruce takes you through previous events, current events, and events to come, I'm confident that you'll discover what multitudes have sensed: Jesus is coming soon!

Through *The Prophetic Promise of the Seventh Day*, God is pouring out new wine unlike any you have *never* tasted. As you drink it in and apply the truths Dr. Bruce shares, you'll come to a deeper place of supernatural faith and a more intimate supernatural walk with Jesus.

Multitudes in the body of Christ, including myself, have yearned to fulfill God's divine plan but struggled as the arm of the flesh tries to rise up and *make* God's work come to pass. As a result, I believe the way in which we've represented Christ on the earth has left much to be desired. But you'll soon hear good news through Dr. Allen's teachings! On the Seventh Day, the Bride of Christ will rise up to demonstrate the miraculous power of God, not through the feeble arm of the flesh, but through the miracle working power of God. On the Seventh Day, we will no longer strive to fulfill His plan! And like God, on the Seventh Day, we will fulfill God's plan from a place of rest. Now that's good news!

Therese Marszalek, Author
Extraordinary Miracles in the Lives of Ordinary People
(Harrison House)

Preface

O ver the years as I've watched prophetic events foretold in the Bible come to pass I've always had a lingering question in my heart: How will the last generation function under such dire circumstances that are portrayed throughout the pages of Scripture?

This question caused me to search the Scriptures over the years for answers and insights. In *The Prophetic Promise of the Seventh Day* I share some of the insights and understanding the Lord has revealed to me in this quest.

Without a doubt, we are living in a very prophetic season pregnant and almost overdue with the promise of fulfillment. Events are quickly unfolding and nations are being positioned both politically and spiritually to enact the final scenes of history. Within this dynamic we have the Body of Christ being prepared and aligned by the Holy Spirit to fulfill its destiny in becoming mature children of God.

With this in mind and with our hearts fixed on the will of the Lord being accomplished in our generation, we are positioned to move in the power of God in unimaginable ways to the extent of literally bringing heaven to earth and seeing a generation transformed and redeemed out of darkness into His glorious light! We are on the threshold of the greatest outpouring of the Spirit of God and the greatest harvest this world has ever known. Not only will we be witness to this, we will be center stage as the fulfillment of every covenant promise in the Word of God comes to pass!

My prayer as you read this is that you find hope and gain insight into your profound destiny during this prophetic season. You are not here by accident. Your worth to the King and the kingdom are inestimable! You are needed for the Body of Christ to fully function in the fullness of authority and liberty we have been called to. It is time to arise and take your place in the army of God and in the Body of Christ and to go forth in victory toward your eternal destiny!

Bruce Allen

CHAPTER 1

The Promise

Quite often, Scripture gives us insights into the times or seasons we as a people find ourselves facing. Right now, the nations are in a season of extraordinary upheaval with many indicators and signs pointing toward a final climatic series of events.

For years I've studied God's Word with a heart to know and understand the Lord and His ways—not just as a God who bestows blessings on those who trust in Him; not just as a giver of gifts; but as a God who desires a relationship with His people more than we've ever understood and comprehended.

It has been through this passionate pursuit of intimacy with the Lord that I began to see deeper levels of revelation in the Word. I began noticing patterns and numeric insights embedded in the Word that speak to us profoundly and with great clarity, not only revealing the heart and character of God Himself, but also speaking to us prophetically regarding the hour in which we live and of things to come.

The more fascinated I became and the more I studied and researched, the more astounded I became until I realized that the very thing I had desired and longed for—a deeper relationship with the Lord—was unfolding in my life.

The Bible clearly teaches in Luke 8:10 that it has been given unto us to know the mysteries of the Kingdom of God. In discovering and learning about the mysteries of the Kingdom of God we invariably begin to discover who the God of the Kingdom is in a deeper and more meaningful way.

In 1999, the Lord began to reveal to me a significant insight in the Scriptures that speaks to this generation and this season we find ourselves in. I am continually amazed as I have studied and taught this revelation by the surprising speed at which it seems to be coming to pass. The first part of this revelation is explained in my previous book, *Promise of the Third Day* published by Destiny Image. We will be examining the second aspect of this revelation relating to the Seventh Day.

> *But, beloved, do not forget this one thing, that with the Lord one day is as a thousand years, and a thousand years as one day* (2 Peter 3:8).

"Don't forget this one thing?" (see 2 Pet. 3:8). After all Peter taught up to this point in his life, he admonishes his hearers to remember "this one thing." Why was this statement of such importance to him? I believe part of the revelation is to be found in the fact that the subject of his statement, *"that with the Lord one day is as a thousand years, and a thousand years as one day" points to a generation…this generation* (see 2 Pet. 3:8). Let's examine why.

If one day is as "a thousand years," from the perspective of eternity, Jesus has really only been gone for two days! God's reference as far as time and eternity is vastly different from ours.

From the time of Jesus until the turn of the century, we have just completed two days (two thousand years), and we are now early in the morning on the third day. Historically, we can go back four thousand years from Jesus to the time of Adam. So from Adam until the turn of the century, we have now completed 6,000 years or six days, and we are early in the morning on the Seventh Day. We can see an unprecedented confluence or an overlapping of the Third Day and the Seventh Day during this millennium.

Israel's Season and Signs

The Third Day and the Seventh Day are profoundly prophetic, unlike any other time in the history of the world, and, obviously, it will never happen again. Not only that, we also see something prophetic that is taking place in Israel. The Word says Jesus was asked by his disciples, "*Lord, when will all these things be and when will they happen?*" (see Matt. 24:3). In Matthew 24:25 and in Luke 21, Jesus began to tell them about seasons and times and things to look for at the end age just prior to His return.

In another passage, Jesus rebuked the Pharisees because they were not able to discern the *"signs of the times"* (Matt. 16:3). This word used for "times" is the Greek word *kairos*—a word which is most often interpreted as "seasons." We can understand from this rebuke that Jesus was teaching that prophetic seasons have a *mark* or *sign* that initiates that season and alludes to the prophetic significance of that season. Were we to take the time to examine every passage of Scripture that deals with times and seasons and their fulfillment, we would be writing an encyclopedia rather than a book. Suffice it to say, we are in a time when hidden secrets in the Word of God will be revealed and hidden mysteries resolved. We have come to a unique "time" and "season" in the history of humankind.

Scripture states that the generation which sees Israel become a nation will not pass away until these things that He refers to come to pass (see Luke 21:32). I have always been taught and I understood that a biblical generation was 40 years. The Hebrew prophets have made it abundantly clear that Jerusalem is a key to Christ's second coming. Scripture states that the city of Jerusalem will become the center of attention during the time of the end.

In Psalm 102:13,16 King David says it this way:

You will arise and have mercy on Zion; For the time to favor her, yes, the set time, has come (Psalm 102:13).

For the Lord shall build up Zion; He shall appear in His glory (Psalm 102:16).

Contrary to current political rhetoric Jerusalem has been Israel's capital since King David established his throne there over 3,000 years ago. It has been destroyed and rebuilt eight times and has changed hands over 27 times. Since A.D. 70 the Jews have not had control over the city.

On May 15, 1948, when the rebirth of the nation of Israel occurred, things seemed to have changed. Jerusalem was declared to be the capital of Israel once again; however, the city was divided. The western half of the city belonged to the Jews and the eastern half was controlled by the Jordanians, to include the Mount of Olives, the Garden of Gethsemane, the Kidron Valley, the Temple Mount, and the Western Wall.

There was a giant cement wall with barbed wire that ran down the middle of the city that was declared to be "No Man's Land." The major problem with this for those of us who look to the Scriptures as the road map by which we can understand biblical prophecy is that beyond "No Man's Land" lay the most sacred area in all of Israel—Mt. Zion. This rendered the prophetic word of Psalms 102 unable to be fulfilled until yet another future date.

During the Six Day War in 1967, Israel reunited the ancient city of Jerusalem. It tore down the cement wall between east and west and Israel now has an undivided capital, including Mt. Zion. Now from June 1967 until June 2007 we see a completion of a 40-year cycle. I sincerely believe that this generation that has seen Jerusalem reunited is the generation that will not pass away until all things are fulfilled! This generation that is witnessing the building up of Zion is the generation that will see Jesus appear. We are in a profoundly prophetic season unlike any this world has ever experienced!

In relation to this, we have the Third Day and the Seventh Day simultaneously being fulfilled in our generation. Israel is now a nation with Jerusalem as its seat of government. This generation is beginning to see prophecy fulfilled at an accelerated rate. Even now as I sit and write, world powers are trying to divide Jerusalem, and we will increasingly see Scripture being fulfilled again and again in our lifetime.

The Days of the Messiah

Interestingly, in Luke 20 the Lord says something about this season that we are in. In my studies on the Seventh Day, I found some very interesting historical tidbits, if you will. Jewish oral tradition has always fascinated me because it releases insight and revelation into the heart of God. In Jewish oral tradition they have always understood God having said that Adam, our father, was only given a six-day stewardship on this earth. That is their understanding, and orally they have passed this down from generation to generation.

Also, in the Talmud it says *"The world as we know it will exist for 6,000 years. The first 2,000 will be chaos. The second 2,000 will mark the years of the Torah and the final 2,000 will include the Messianic age.*"[1]

Isn't it interesting and significant that we see an event that occurs as a demarcation line moving us from one 2,000-year cycle/season into another 2,000-year cycle/season? The first two days, or 2,000-year span, were considered to be the days of chaos. In other words, from the creation of Adam until Abraham leaving Ur of the Chaldeans, it was chaotic. Sin was in control. The Adamic covenant was in force, yet had been rejected by the nations. So the Lord chose Abram that in him God could establish a covenant and bring order to His creation.

The second set of two days, or 2,000 years, were the days of the Torah, or law. This takes us from the birth of Isaac (the promised seed) to the birth of Jesus (the Promised Seed). The third and last 2,000-year span covers the time from the resurrection of Jesus to this present day. I had always wondered, since I first got saved at 14, why the Scripture always says "the last days" in the New Testament? It was and is speaking about the days of Messiah, Jesus, which completes six days, or 6,000 years.

Hippolytus, an early Church leader (A.D. 170-236) wrote: *"And 6,000 years must needs be accomplished, in order that the Sabbath may come, the rest, the holy day, on which God rested from all of his works..."*

Period of Prophetic Transition

Other Church fathers believed the story of Elijah gave another hint to the 6,000 years attributed to the stewardship of humankind on this earth. In First Kings 19:18 it says, *"Yet, I have left me seven thousand in Israel, all the knees which have not bowed unto Baal, and every mouth which hath not kissed him"* (KJV). Now this is fascinating: the belief was that because Elijah was to come before the great and terrible day of the Lord (see Mal. 4:5), the 7,000 prophets pointed or hinted to the fact that the day of the Lord would come at the end of the 6,000 years of humanity's stewardship on this earth, or at the beginning of the seventh millennium. At that point, the Lord is going to establish a Kingdom reign on this earth, a millennial reign of Christ where He will rule and reign for a thousand years. Since the reign of Christ spoken of in Revelation 20:4 is one thousand years, then the 1,000 years can correlate to one day (see 1 Pet. 2:8) in God's sight (this one day or the millennium relates to the Lord's day). Since the millennial reign is said to be a time of rest and peace, we can see that it correlates with the Seventh Day of creation where God rested and ceased from His labors.

We are right now at the point of transition from the sixth day to the seventh day, where God is releasing the promise of the fulfillment of these prophecies into the hearts and minds of His people all over the world. Wherever we travel, there are people who have a divine dissatisfaction and a stirring in their spirit. They know this is a very portentous and prophetic time, a time of profound destiny to which each of us has been called by God Himself.

In the New Testament, there is a parable that alludes to this very same 6,000-year timetable and its fulfillment. This concept was so real to the Jewish mind-set that Jesus taught a parable based on this 6,000-year stewardship principle. In Luke 20:9-16 Jesus began to tell the people this parable:

> *"A certain man planted a vineyard, leased it to vine dressers, and went into a far country for a long time. Now at vintagetime he sent a servant to the vinedressers, that they might give him some of the fruit of the vineyard, but the vine dressers beat him and sent him away empty-handed. Again he sent another servant; and they beat him also, treated him shamefully, and*

sent him away empty-handed. Again he sent a third; and they wounded him also, and cast him out. Then the owner of the vineyard said 'what should I do? I will send my beloved son. Probably they will respect him when they see him.' But when the vinedressers saw him, they reasoned among themselves saying, 'This is the heir come let us kill him, that the inheritance may be ours.' So they cast him out of the vineyard and killed him. Therefore what will the owner of the vineyard do to them? He will come and destroy those vinedressers and give the vineyard to others."And when they heard it they said, "Certainly not!" (Luke 20:9-16).

There are two applications here. First he was talking about Israel and the Gentiles. God had given the covenant promise of Abraham to the Jewish people, and they had killed and despised His prophets and were about to crucify the Son. So He was going to give that promise, this vineyard and the Word of God to other vinedressers who are the Gentile nations until the fullness of time had come.

Second, the Scripture refers to the parable of the six days that Adam had to rule and reign on this earth before the Seventh Day when God the Father was going to come back and establish His Kingdom through Jesus the Messiah. That is exactly where we find ourselves; we are in a period of transition. It is an extraordinary time! Jesus was with the woman at the well in Samaria when He spoke prophetically, revealing her whole life. She went back into Samaria and exclaimed to everyone about all that Jesus had said. By the time she was finished, she brought the whole of Samaria to Jesus. Jesus remained there for two days, and on the third day he went back to his people Israel (see John 4). This is yet another picture of the fullness of time being fulfilled in our generation.

A remarkable awakening is taking place in Israel in this hour as their eyes are opened to the truth of the Gospel accounts of

Jesus! They will know Him, the crucified Messiah. Thousands of Jewish people are coming to a saving knowledge of Jesus Christ right now because they are having a supernatural encounter with Jesus.

Interpreting Moshe's Dream

Here is a modern-day example: a man named Moshe in Tel Aviv was 71 years old when the following story happened. (He would be approximately 76 or 77 now.) In a period of 90 days he had the exact same dream over 20 times, and it disturbed him greatly. He was distraught; he didn't know what to do. So he went to every rabbi he knew, because he was a very devout Jewish man. He had a store in Tel Aviv and he would ask every customer and every friend, "Can you tell me what this dream means?" Nobody could interpret his dream. One day there was a March for Jesus group coming down the street and he was so desperate he was even willing to talk to Christians! So he ran out and grabbed a man, and said, "Please sir, can you interpret this dream for me?"

The man replied, "Well, I don't know, what is your dream?"

Moshe began to share the dream with him. He said, "In my dream, I was awakened in the middle of the night by a loud trumpet blast, and when I ran to my front door and opened it, there stood Gabriel with a trumpet to his mouth and he was blowing it. Thousands of people were being caught up into the air. And there was a man on a white horse, and he had on a crown and a sword was coming out of his mouth, and on his breastplate it said "The Conqueror." Please, sir, can you tell me what that means?"

Unbeknownst to Moshe, this man was a pastor, and he opened his Bible to First Corinthians chapter 15 and told Moshe, "Read this."

As Moshe began to read *"In a moment, in the twinkling of an eye at the last trump the dead in Christ shall arise first..."* (see 1 Cor. 15:52) upon which he began to dance, and sing and praise God and weep right in the middle of the street. He said, "That's my dream! That's my dream!" This pastor had the privilege of leading Moshe to the Lord right there, and to this day Moshe is anticipating that at any moment there is going to be a trumpet blast calling the Church away to ever be with the Lord.

(For more documented visions and visitations like these, see *The Jesus Visions—Miracles Among Muslims* by Christine Darg, published by Destiny Image.)[2]

This is not an isolated incident. There are devout Hasidic rabbis who are having face-to-face encounters with Jesus, but the Lord has been telling them, "Don't come out of the closet yet; stay where you are—study and await My call. I will speak and tell you, 'Now!' when it is time, and you will stand up to say, 'Jesus is truly the Messiah.'" All over the world, encounters similar to this are happening on an unprecedented scale. There has never been a day like this one.

The Seventh-Day Promise

This is the Seventh Day—the day of the regrafting of the Jews into the Body—and it will be woven into everything you see. You will see that on the Seventh Day, it was Jesus' custom to enter into the synagogue and teach. What He did was reveal Himself to God's covenant people. On this Seventh Day, Jesus is revealing Himself in the synagogue, in the temples, in homes. All over Israel and the world, Jesus is revealing Himself to His people. Bible prophecy is being fulfilled, whether we understand it or not. It is being fulfilled in ways we neither thought possible nor even conceived.

We live in a profoundly prophetic time. God is pulling out all the stops. The number *seven* in Scripture, in biblical numerology, is acknowledged as the number of "rest and completion." It indicates covenant promise fulfilled. It is also considered to be God's sacred number. It is commonly used when the Lord is emphasizing a pattern for completion, fulfillment, or a spiritual truth. Every covenant promise in the Bible is going to be fulfilled on this day. As you study the prophetic significance of the Seventh Day, you will find that every promise was completed and fulfilled early in the morning on the Seventh Day. We are in the very midst of seeing these promises fulfilled in our generation. Right now, you are a "terminal" generation. I'm not saying "terminal" in the sense of dying, but rather in the sense of being a generation that will see the fulfillment of all things promised us by God. This is the final act, and the curtains are about to go down on the current world system.

Miracle of the Enoch Generation

Jude 14 says you are an Enoch generation. Enoch was the seventh generation from Adam, and he experienced a supernatural, bodily translation into Heaven. We are presently the seventh millennium (Seventh Day removed) from Adam. Just as Enoch escaped natural death through supernatural intervention from Heaven, this generation of believers will experience a transference to Heaven called the "catching away" or the "gathering together." This is the generation that is going to see Jesus return. This is the generation that is going to hear the final great trumpet blast. I could tell you about Arabs, Muslims, Jews, Buddhists, atheists, and agnostics all over the world, who are experiencing face-to-face encounters with Jesus, and He's telling them, "I'm the way, the truth, and the life, follow Me," and they are getting gloriously saved.

God ceased work on the Seventh Day of re-creation, not from fatigue, but from achievement. Hear this with a prophetic ear: God ceased His work on this day, not from fatigue, but because of completion. Everything that He began is going to be completed on this day. Faithful is He who called you who also shall do it. He who began a good work in you is going to complete it. When? Today on this Seventh Day!

Every promise you have had from God is going to see fulfillment in this day. It's not going to take years, as it has in the past, for the fulfillment of those prophetic promises. Prophetic words are coming to pass at an accelerated rate because it is the end of the age. This is the time that every prophet has long desired to see. They longed to look into the mystery of Christ, yet their desire was to see the culmination and fulfillment of their respective prophetic words being fulfilled.

One of the challenges the Lord has placed before me is in studying about transportation/translation by faith and believing for it in our generation. (I like to refer to it as "Phillip Airlines" based on the story in Acts chapter 8.) We have had some experiences, and God has taken us deeper and deeper into the Word regarding this subject (to be written about in a later book). Furthermore, I believe this next couple of years will see this type of supernatural experience becoming more the norm rather than the exception. With all my heart, I believe this. Not only has the Lord been speaking this to my heart, but to many others we've met throughout our travels in various nations. I believe one of the major reasons the Lord is about to release this miracle to the Body of Christ is because the time is short and we have tasks to accomplish for our King before His return. In a moment you could suddenly be in Jerusalem, Judea, Samaria, or the uttermost parts of the earth, and then home in time for dinner. (Unless you want dinner in another nation, of course.)

It is the last day. It is the last moment of history, and you have an extraordinary destiny. If you think you are an accident, then you have discredited God. You are not an accident. You are not here by mistake. You are here because you have a divine purpose and a destiny. You are going to see a move of God unlike anything this world has ever experienced. Not only are you going to see it, you're going to participate in it. This is the moment all of creation has been awaiting: the hour of the coming forth of the mature sons of God.

ENDNOTES

1. Michael L. Rodkinson, ed., trans, *New Edition of the Babylonian Talmud.* Volumes I-X. (1903).

2. Christine Darg, *Miracles Among Muslims* (Pescara, IT: Destiny Image Europe Publishers, 2007).

Chapter 2

Sanctification and Consecration

It is time for us to stop trying to play Church, figure out how to do Church, and talk like the Church. It is time for us to *be* the Church. It is time to recognize that we are set apart—*sanctified*—to do the Father's work. That can only happen as we come to the place of absolute surrender, and absolute surrender is the doorway to rest. Not everything that has been done in the past was all wrong, not by any stretch of the imagination. We have used the gifts and tools that God has given us, and we walked in the understanding we had to the best of our ability. However, the Lord is releasing greater revelation and insight today for us to begin to walk in something the world has never seen.

On this Seventh Day, I see us coming to a place in our lives similar to where Paul said *"I no longer live by my faith, but I live by the faith of the Son of God"* (see Gal. 2:20). It is time to get beyond our concept of faith and beyond our own human ability to grab hold of God. Instead, we need to be divested of our fleshly attempts at spirituality and come to the place where our concepts, our life, is hidden in Christ. We, like the apostles, must become dead and buried in Christ and live by the faith of the Son of God instead of our own meager faith. In that place, nothing is impossible. Nothing!

In John 14:12, Jesus said *"The works that I do, [you] will do also; and greater works than these [you] will do, because I go to my father."* Notice the Scripture says "the works that I *do*" not "the works that I *did*." There are two functions Jesus has in Heaven; did you know that? The first is to prepare a place for us as our Bridegroom. Jesus said, *"I go to prepare a place for you"* (John 14:2). He is the Bridegroom who prepares a house for you. The second thing He is doing right now is interceding—or standing in the gap before the Father for us. *"He ever [lives] to make intercession"* (Heb. 7:25 KJV). There are only two things Scripture says that Jesus does today: He is making a place ready for you, and He is interceding for you. If we are going to do the works He is doing, then we must prepare a place for Him, and we must be yielded enough to intercede as His heart desires.

It was not long ago the Lord asked me if I would be willing to yield my tongue to Him that He could pray the purposes of God released on the earth. As I submitted my will to Him in this, I found that seasons of intercession would come upon me, and I have literally spent days praying in the Spirit until the Lord released me.

What is the place He wants you to prepare for Him? It is your heart. If He lives in you, and all of creation was created through Him, then the works that He did, you can do! *"Most assuredly, I say to you, he who believes in Me, the works that I do he will do also; and greater works than these he will do, because I go to My Father"* (John 14:12).

We have had a measure of understanding of this because we know the power of our words. At least we say we do. But we rarely actually practice what we think we know. Otherwise, most of us wouldn't ever talk! Everything He created was created by Him *speaking*, and in the same manner we have been enabled and commissioned by the Lord to operate in the same fashion—to create through what we speak. We are going to see a release of creative miracles that are going to astound the world. I don't just mean creative miracles in our physical bodies; I mean creative miracles in the natural that are going to cause the world to sit up and take notice. Ask yourself this question: "What am I believing for?" The Lord has been challenging me time and time again to believe for things I've never seen and for things I've never heard.

Some are content to hang on until Jesus comes and then escape before difficulties overpower them. However, there are a growing number of believers who are hungering for more than just the *status quo* of the modern-day Christian experience. For many, we have been in the position to receive His promises, but we have not possessed them. We've stated what we believe and even what the Word says about us, and yet many of the promises of God seem elusive and unattainable to us. Why? I believe it is because the Church as a whole hasn't been mature enough to adequately handle the release of much of what the Word promises. Three (Third Day) is the number of completion and maturity. Seven (Seventh Day) is the number of completion, covenant promise fulfilled, and rest. A transition is taking place in this season in the Body of Christ that will see a measure of maturity not witnessed in the corporate Body of Christ and a completion of the plans and purposes of God. What He began in you, He is going to complete. That promise is for now, not just eternity!

Becoming One...With the Father

Something keeps resounding in my spirit and it is what Jesus spoke in John 10:30: "*I and My Father are one.*" This statement has been stirring me, and I've continually asked, "Lord, what does that look like?" We see it written in the Gospels, but what does that really look like operatively in the life of the believer? I do know that a facet of this is His calling of us to a place of intimacy with both He and the Father—a place of "oneness" with the Godhead. We saw a picture of that in Christ who was the personification of the Father on the earth. Yet, there is a gulf between what we know, what we sense, and what we really walk in. On this Seventh Day, this day of rest and completion, we are going to *know* what it means to be wholly given over to the Father and the Son with no more pretense and no more religious props—but a total divesting ourselves of carnal fleshly appetites and desires and a complete union of rest with Him. Can you imagine a whole body of believers saying in fact, "I and my Father are one!" Positionally, that is true, because He is in us and we are in Him, but we do not actually model the fullness of the revelation of that statement here in our lives. Most of the Church lives like hell but says, "We are going to Heaven."

Four Divine Acts

There were clearly four divine acts attributed to the work of God on the Seventh Day. The *first* is that God ended His work. There was a divine completion and perfection. Hear this again— hear with a prophetic ear: *There are four divine acts that are going to take place in the lives of each individual believer, in the corporate Church, in the world, and throughout all of history, and all of creation on this Seventh Day.* Four divine acts. Again the first act was God ended His work. He said, "It is finished" (John 19:30). Corporately, we are within sight of the finish line.

The *second* act God did was that God rested. He ceased from all of His exertions. Exertion speaks of sweat, the labor of the flesh, and of us doing rather than us being. We have been seeing this more frequently in our ministry all over the world in the testimonies of other people. Jesus said, "*The things I can do you can do also*" (see John 14:12). Then in John 5:19, He says "*I only do what I see the Father do*" (author's paraphrase). Reading this, I said, "Man, I've been robbed blind." Literally! You see, it's your birthright to see. Jesus said, "What I can do, you can do, and I only do what I see."

Let me give you one definition of rest from my life and experience. I've been in many meetings where I have had open visions of the presence of angels as well as the Lord Jesus Himself. There are times when we have had individuals come for prayer and before I have a chance to pray I see the answer. One such occasion was in a meeting in Kettle Falls, Washington, in 2007. We had a gentleman come forward for prayer. He wanted to be healed of terminal cancer in his lungs. We knew this man and had prayed for him and this condition on various occasions, as had other ministers in the local area. As this brother was explaining to me what he wanted prayer for, I saw an angel with a silver platter enter the back of the Church and walk up to him. As I waited upon the Lord to see what He was doing by means of His messenger, I saw this angel reach into the chest cavity of this man and I heard as well as saw this angel pull out this large dark mass of putrefying flesh. I heard in vivid "surround sound" the sucking noise and the splat as he slapped it down upon the silver platter. The angel then looked at me, walked to the back of the room once again and I saw him throw this mass out. He nodded at me and left.

I told this gentleman what I had seen and I said, "I don't have to pray for you now; I am just going to agree with what I saw the Lord doing." He received that word, and on Tuesday of that very week he went back to his doctor and after a series of tests was pronounced to be cancer-free.

That is rest! That is true rest. It does not take human effort. You don't have to stir it up, mix it up, or make it up. You just agree with what the Lord is doing, and if He's not doing anything you sit down and be quiet. There is a place for acting on the Word and I am not negating that. I am saying we are coming into a season of interaction with the supernatural realm to such an extent that we will adhere to the example of Jesus and be able to do what we see as well as what we hear.

I fully believe we are about to see a new and radical Church coming forth and being released in the earth. This Church will be so enamored of God, so fused together with His heart and character that they are not going to do anything without seeing God do it first. They will be as bold as lions. They will be as wise as serpents and as harmless as doves. They are not going to say, "Well, that looks like a good idea, let's do it. This is the way we've always done church." No. They are just going to say, "Lord, I cease from all my works. What are you doing?"

We will be tempted as in the past by sister Squirmy and brother Irritable who in their religious zeal and lack of rest will say, "Come on, what kind of church is this? We have to do something." However in this season, because our hearts and minds are fixed on Him, we will not be moved into fleshly action; we will remain in rest. And the *something* we *have to do* will be to cease from our own works, rest, and wait on God!

The *third* thing God did was to bless the Seventh Day. It is a divine invocation, a speaking forth of the heart of the Father into this day, into your life, into this generation, and into this period of seeming uncertainty. The Lord is speaking blessing into this generation like no other generation. This is the hour we are going to see the blessings of Abraham overtake us. You are not going to have to give to receive. Giving will become a matter of the heart and it will be a delight. We are going to understand we are nothing more than stewards. Everything we have belongs to Him. It is not ours in the first place. If He says give away your house, we will say,

"Lord this is your house; who do you want me to give it to?" It is not going to be, "Oh my goodness, where am I going to live? What am I going to do?" No, we will say "Yes, Lord." That is rest. Knowing my Daddy will take care of me.

You know what is going to liberate some of us into this place of complete rest? We are going to see what He has prepared for us. You will look at this world and what it has to offer—all of its bobbles and trinkets, all of its *bling*— and you will say, "This doesn't interest me anymore." Why? Because you will have seen what the Lord has prepared for you, and this world will no longer hold sway over your appetites and desires. I have never seen the righteous forsaken, or His seed begging for bread (see Ps. 37:25). I have never seen God be tight-fisted with His covenant blessings when we learn to trust and rest in Him. I have never seen God withhold good when it is due those that are His (see Ps. 84:11). He is not stingy and He doesn't do that. We are in the season of the release of the resources of Heaven upon those that are desiring His Kingdom to come and His will to be done. God is speaking blessing to this generation and it is overtaking us. Let that reverberate in your heart right now. The blessings of God are going to overtake you, overwhelm you, and you will not be able to contain them! We must remember, we are part of a Kingdom that cannot be shaken! Do not live your life based on a steady diet of CNN or Fox News. Base your life on God and His Word!

This is the day you will reap blessing where you have never sown. Watch and see! It's already begun because that is the Covenant of Abraham, and it will overtake this generation.

The *fourth* thing God did was to sanctify the Seventh Day. He separated and dedicated it for His purpose. The Lord is going to complete the work He began in you. He is going to bring you to a place of rest in this generation and in this hour. The Lord is going to bless you so much you can hardly stand yourself. Then God is going to sanctify you and set you apart because you have a divine destiny and purpose in this generation. He has already been at work in you, and He is going to complete it so that you can fulfill your destiny.

Seasons of Supernatural Refreshing

So God ceased the work of creation on the Seventh Day, not from fatigue, but from achievement. He had completed His work and was refreshed. There are times of refreshing that are coming from the presence of the Lord. It has never been truer than in this hour, in this day. What does refreshing from the Lord look like? It is an infusion of the very life of God into our mortal bodies that quickens this mortal body. It is the same infusion of supernatural strength that Elijah experienced when he outran Ahab's chariot (see 1 Kings 18:46). It is the same infusion of supernatural strength that allowed Elijah to go for 40 days in strength by eating the meal the angel brought to him (1 Kings 19:5-8). We shall also outrun chariots. We will run through a troop and leap over a wall. We will do exploits for God beyond our natural ability.

> ...but the people who know their God shall be strong, and carry out great exploits (Daniel 11:32).

God the Father chose us with purpose and destiny in mind, and that fact alone should overwhelm us. Remember in school when you had gym class and you were to play team sports? The coach would choose two captains and they in turn would choose their prospective teams? Do you remember that sometimes having been picked, you felt lucky—especially when picked by the team you knew would win? Well, the Lord chose you, and you were His first pick, His "A" team! How do I know that? Because before the foundation of the world He had you in mind for this day, this last inning, with this purpose in mind: for you to see and participate in the completion and fulfillment of all that He began to do from the beginning of time. This is your destiny!

> *It is a sign between Me and the children of Israel forever; for in six days the Lord made the heavens and the earth, and on the Seventh Day He rested and was refreshed* (Exodus 31:17).

Men and women are likewise told to rest and refresh themselves on the Seventh Day, after six days of work. For 6,000 years we have tried to accomplish the plans, purposes, and the destiny God has for our lives with our own strength and with our own carnal, finite minds. Some of what has been done has been spirit and some of it has been flesh. In that mixture you never find the fullness of what God wants to release in the earth. Flesh and spirit are like oil and water; they don't mix, even when you shake them up. But we have entered a season now where God is going to release that substance called rest. God is going to supernaturally invest in us this deposit of rest so that we will be able to cease from our own works and rely wholly on Him.

Running the Distance

When I was in high school, I became a distance runner. I loved to run! I would run miles and miles, most of the time putting in at least 110 miles every week. Every time I would run a race, either a one-mile or two-mile race (somehow the two mile seemed to work better for me), I would come around that last 440 and know the finish line was there. I would dig deep for every last vestige of strength and stamina I could muster. Many times I remember thinking, "I don't know if I can do this; I'm going to pass out, or die, or something." But when you're in a race, you dig deep because you see the finish line and you press on until you've crossed that finish line. That is where I see the Church right now. We are within sight of the finish line, and we must dig deep for every last ounce of courage and stamina we have and press on toward that finish line. We must abandon ourselves and our own selfish agendas to the purposes of God for this generation.

It is time to dig deep. It is time to take everything that is within you—all the passion, all the fire, all the love, all the hope, all the joy, everything that God has birthed within you—and dig deep and bring it forth. The finish line is in sight. It is no time to be reticent and sit back on our "blessed assurance" and say, "Well, I'm not sure about this." (For those who don't know what I mean by "sitting on your blessed assurance," that is a euphemism for sitting on our lazy behinds!) My grandfather once told my dad, "It is better to aim for the stars and miss, than to aim for the garbage can and hit." I am saying, go for it! Go for the gold! Give it all you've got!

Here is another aspect of rest: I can trust The Father whether I make a mistake or not. He is with me. I'm blessed. Let me really throw you a shocker. Do you know it is almost impossible to fail in God? How do I know that? There is only one failure with God from which you cannot recover: falling down and staying down instead of getting back up. You wind up wallowing in that place of failure; however, if you get back up, dust off your clothes, repent, and drive on, you haven't failed. You see, in God's economy, it never happened! The blood of Jesus eradicated and washed away that sin and you are now free to progress toward your destiny. You have learned from your experience, and now you move on.

So you see, in the Christian walk, if you walk humbly before God, you can't fail! The quicker you learn to repent and get back in the game, the more you are released into a discerning and understanding of the heart of the Father. Don't be afraid of making mistakes. If you must nurture fear (although that is sin), be afraid of doing nothing. Mistakes won't kill you, sitting on your *blessed assurance* will. Believe me when I tell you, there are no couch potatoes in Heaven!

One of the most sacred words in the Bible is the word *kadosh*, which means "holy." It is said that this word, perhaps more than any other, conveys not only the mystery but the majesty of God. It carries tremendous importance. *Kadosh* is a fascinating study and should you choose to study this, you will see the different nuances of its meaning. It is note-worthy to realize that the very first time *Kadosh* is found in the Scripture, it is not speaking of a location or even a person or a place, but it is speaking of a time.

Genesis 2:3 says, *God blessed the seventh day and made it holy* (NIV).

This Seventh Day is holy to God. It is set apart. It is sanctified. It is separated unto God for His purpose. *It is holy!*

The Law of First Mention

We find a significant principle in the study of interpreting Scriptures called the *Law of First Mention*. Simply stated, it is this: The first time something is mentioned in Scripture, in context, from that point on, you can use this first mention as a basis to interpret all other Scriptures that speak of the same subject.

With that in mind, then the first usage of the word *holy* or *Kadosh* takes on an even greater significance. The very first time that word *holy* is used, it is used about a day— the Seventh Day. Every other Scripture that alludes to the word *holy* in context, points back to a certain day with a vivid prophetic significance. We could actually go through the Scriptures and take every place the word *holy* is used and find that it is going to point to something on or about the Seventh Day that God is going to do sovereignly and supernaturally or it will prophetically speak to the character of His people who are coming forth in this generation.

This day is holy to God. I want to share something with you about sanctification. *Sanctification* is a separation from a profane to a sacred purpose. It is consecration. It literally means a separation unto God from a profane, secular, or carnal use to a sacred spiritual use. This Seventh Day of history in the world is a day that is separated unto God from a profane, secular use, or a carnal use to a sacred spiritual use. That means on this Holy Seventh Day there is going to be a supernatural invasion of the realm of the Spirit upon this unsuspecting world. It is a sacred time. It is a set apart time for God to specifically interact with His creation.

Why do you think we are hearing of so many people having a face-to-face encounter with God? It is a Holy Day. It is sacred. It is a day of supernatural interaction between Heaven and earth. Why are we seeing so many people exposed in Christendom because of their secret sins that they thought they could hide from the world? A Holy God is saying, "We can deal with this in the secret place or I will expose it in the market place, but on this day it will be dealt with!" This day is holy to God. You cannot profane this day and get away with it. You do not play church on this day and get away with it. The standard has always been holiness for the people of God (see 1 Peter 1:16), however, on this day there will be an enforcement of that standard by God for those who are called on this holy Day.

A separation is taking place. The Lord is saying this day is holy and we had better regard it as holy. Why? Because *He is* going to complete everything He began in Genesis 1. I can never enter in to the fullness of my destiny until I embrace the fullness of what God says is mine. One of those things is I am called to be holy as He is holy. I am called to be separated from a profane secular lifestyle that is displeasing to God, and I am called to move into a place of a sacred union with God where I become everything He says I am. I can no longer wink at sin, nor can I permit myself the luxury of inactivity in God's Kingdom. I must choose conformity to this Holy God who has called me to be as He is, or I must choose apostasy and conformity to this world. Either way, I must choose!

How do I do that? I make a choice. The Lord taught me years ago that if I would make the choice to be conformed to His Word, He would make the change. That is all I can do. Everything else after that is flesh. "Lord, I'm willing. Be my *able* that I may do Your will. I have made the choice Lord. I choose you." Now I am positioned for God to make the change. We must stop striving in our own strength and rest in Him. Faithful is He who called who also will do it (see 1 Thess. 5:24)!

This is the hour we are in, this Seventh Day, which is holy to the Lord. It demands our attention and our adherence to what He is saying in this time. That means we'd better have our ears attuned to Him as we ask, "Father, what are you saying? What is your heart? What are you doing?"

Do only what He tells you to do in this time! We take principles from the Word, and we make formulas and we think we have the heart of God in our actions. That is called denominationalism. The principle is this: be led of the Spirit, and adhere to the principles of the Word. The principle is that God raises the dead; God heals the sick, so do something by faith! That is the principle of the Word. Be led of the Spirit.

We find no record of anything being called Holy except what God called holy; and the very first mention of Holy was in regard to a day, a place in time. It is the Seventh Day, which is holy. It has been said that the essence of the Seventh Day is detachment from the tyranny of things and the tyranny of earthly preoccupation. We live in this world and we have to do certain things and interact with this world. I am not saying to go live on a mountaintop and chant. I am saying, don't be so immersed and preoccupied with the things of this life that you neglect the weightier things of God. As a matter of fact, let's get to the place where the Lord says, *"See the birds of the air? They don't toil; they don't work. They don't worry about what they are going to eat, where they're going to sleep like you do, oh you of little faith, you must know that my father will take care of all of that"* (see Matt. 6:26-33). We have got to move into a place where we acquiesce to God because it's His business. We do what He tells us to do, and we trust Him to do what He says He will do.

Second Corinthians 6:12 says this: *You are not restricted by us, but you are restricted by your own affections.*

We must become detached from the tyranny of things and the tyranny of earthly preoccupations. Whatever has your attention becomes your restriction or your limitation. That is why the Word says in Colossians 3:2 to *"set your affections on things above, not on things on the earth."* Set your affections on things above. Why? Because you are restricted by your own affections! So, we had better aim for the stars and hit! You have probably heard well-meaning people say, "Don't become so heavenly minded that you're no earthly good?" Actually, Scripture tells us we are "seated in heavenly places." The more heavenly minded you are, the more earthly good you become!

CHAPTER 3

Wisdom from the Ancient Rabbis

The ancient rabbis always taught that the meaning of the Seventh Day is to share in what is eternal and to begin to interact with the eternal realm. You have millions of people all over the world today talking about Heaven invading earth, about visitations of Jesus, visitation of angels, manna from Heaven, gemstones from Heaven, and other remarkable miracles and manifestations of His glory. The increase in all of these manifestations is, I believe, because God has set this Seventh Day aside. It is holy, sanctified, and it has purpose. We are going to begin to interact with what is eternal more than we interact with that which is not eternal.

It's imperative that we have a divine perspective on things. Jesus said in Matthew 14:12, *"The works that I do, [you] shall do also."* Not the works that He did. Its present tense. We keep trying to do what He did. That has its place. We have to start somewhere, but what is He doing today? I know He is going from Heaven to earth visiting millions of people, preaching the Gospel and saying follow me: *"I am the way the truth and the life"* (see John 14:6). Lord, if you can do that, then I can do that. Why? God's Word says so. How about walking on water? Some friends of my wife and I have a boat and we sometimes go boating with them on the lakes around where we live. Many times I say, "Ok, let's give it a shot," and I step out of the boat onto the water putting my faith into practice, just as Jesus and Peter did. To date, all I've progressed in is I am becoming a better swimmer! That doesn't deter me, I just keep practicing because practice makes proficient!

I heard a story about an evangelist in Indonesia who was up in the interior way back in the jungle. He came upon a village and he began to preach the Gospel to them. The people got very angry with this man and his talk of a strange God. They became demonically enraged and began to come after him with clubs, sticks, and knives. Seeing this, he began to run, and as he was running, without forethought, he ran across the lake, as it was the only means of immediate escape! God's man of faith and power shouted, "I'm out of here!" When the villagers saw that, the fear of the Lord came on them and they said, "This man's God is real." God had purpose in it, and it didn't take a whole lot of faith. His purpose was accomplished and the entire village got saved!

The Mystery of the Creation

The ancient rabbis also taught about this Seventh Day—that it is time to turn from the results of creation to the mystery of creation, from the world that has been created, to the Creator of the world.

And He said, "to you it has been given to know the mysteries of the kingdom of God...." (Luke 8:10).

What is the mystery of creation? What is this mystery that we are talking about? The mysteries of creation that some are learning in quantum physics is that everything they are discovering is already in the Bible. They are quantifying it, but it is already there in the Word! God is releasing in the Seventh Day understanding of the mysteries of creation and everything He spoke.

Creation is summed up in the Word. He upholds all things by the Word of His power. Did you know they found that below the nucleus of an atom, or proton, the thing that holds all of that together is sound? They have discovered the unifying factor in all of this is a sound. Now that is fascinating when you realize that Jesus upholds all things by the *Word* of His power. That sound went forth, and it still upholds and holds everything together.

A noted physicist told my wife, Reshma, and I over lunch one day that researchers have found embedded in every DNA strand the ancient Hebrew alphabet. You take the DNA strand and you look at it with a micron microscope and you find embedded in the DNA strand the ancient Hebrew alphabet. Where is that in the Bible? John 1:1: "*In beginning was the Word, and the Word was with God, and the Word was God.*" And John 1:14 "*And the Word became flesh and dwelt among us, and we beheld His glory, the glory as of the only begotten of the Father, full of grace and truth.*"

You are made in His image. Think about that: all that is holding the atoms of your body together is a sound, His Word—what He released in the beginning of creation and what your DNA is made up of. When you speak the Word over your life and your body then your body begins to respond affirmatively to that Word.

During Rosh Hashanah 2006 during a visitation the Lord Jesus handed me a book. I was excited and I said "Lord, what is this book?" and He said, "It is the book of mysteries, revelation that I have reserved for the end of the age and for the people in this generation." He went on to tell me that this generation is being granted the privilege of receiving the unveiling of these great mysteries because of the fullness of time and the season we are in.

The rabbis taught that on the Seventh Day it is time to move into an understanding of the mysteries of this creation. This is moving from the results of creation to the mystery of creation. The book of mysteries has been given to you to understand and know the mysteries of the Kingdom of God. If we thought that the book was just about Jesus coming to earth and shedding His blood, we've missed much more than we can imagine. The Bible is a continual unveiling of the character and majesty of God.

A Passion for His Presence

The rabbis taught that the Seventh Day was to demand all of humankind's attention to a single-minded devotion of total love toward God. How do we see that being reflected in this Seventh Day? For the last ten years, as we have traveled around the world, we have witnessed an increase in a hunger and passion for the Lord. There has been what I call a "divine dissatisfaction" birthed in the hearts of God's people and an increased passion for more of Him. This passion that burns in the heart of God's people is a profound indicator of the urgency of the hour and the season in which we find ourselves. Why do I say that? The Scripture teaches us in Psalm 37:4 that if we will delight ourselves in the Lord that the Lord will give us the desire of our heart, and He did just that, birthing within His people a greater passion and desire for Him.

We are in a profound prophetic time in God. Again, the ancient rabbis have said that the Seventh Day is the greatest and most precious gift humankind has received from the storehouses of God! They contend that the likeness of God can be found on the Seventh Day. It's a time when people will not see you, but Jesus in you. The likeness of God is going to be found in and upon the people of God on this Seventh Day! His likeness will be found in you because your passion and hunger for more of Him has drawn you into the presence of His glory and caused us to grow from glory to glory, line upon line, precept upon precept, until you have finally been captured by the one who has pursued you: the Lord Himself!

People are going to look at you and recognize that Jesus is in you. For those of us who are desirous to be conformed to the image of Christ, this season will be an ever-increasing time of transformation and passion for our magnificent obsession: Jesus. No other goal is worthy of a man or woman of faith than to be like Him. All else pales in comparison and is not even worthy of mention. The Lord will continue to turn up the dial of passion and hunger for more of Him as we move forward into this Seventh Day, culminating in the greatest harvest the world has ever witnessed just prior to the return of Christ for His own. The opportunity to become everything His Word declares us to be is clearly before us. The Scripture states, *"As He is, so are we in this world"* (1 John 4:17b), and the Word is very clear: It does not say I can do *some* things through Christ who strengthens me, but it says *"I can do all things through Christ"* (Phil. 4:13)!

Preparing for the Bridegroom

Quite frequently in our meetings, the Lord has prompted me to ask a question that on the surface may seem ludicrous, but in reality is very telling. Here is the question: If you knew Jesus was coming back at 9:36 P.M. this evening, would you change your life? If your answer is yes, the way the majority of individuals respond, then there is a gap in your understanding of who God is and what His Word says. We are to be always on the alert for His appearing, and we are to be living each day as if this were the very day He is going to return. We should be ready for His return right now! That is how close He is.

This day, the rabbis said, is to provoke us to think about that place, that realm called eternity where God sits and reigns. As we continue to study the scriptures and see biblical prophecy coming to pass before our very eyes, our hearts and minds should more and more be focused on the nearness and reality of His eternal Kingdom. If our hearts truly long to be with Him we cannot help but to gaze into His Word with longing in our eyes. Our Bridegroom is coming for us!

Proverbs 23:7 says, *For as he thinketh in his heart, so he is* (KJV).

Matthew 22:37 says you should "*love the Lord your God with all your heart, with all your soul, and with all your mind.*" The word *mind* is the Greek word *dianoia* which means "imagination." This is the first commandment with a promise. He is provoking us to set our affections on things above by properly framing pictures of the Kingdom of Heaven in our imaginations.

You are not restricted by us, but you are restricted by your own affections (2 Corinthians 6:12).

The *New International Dictionary of New Testament Theology* states, "When the Greek word *dianoia* is used in relation to the heart, it always means imagination."[1] Isaiah 26:3 says, "*You will keep* him *in perfect peace,* whose *mind is stayed* on You, *because he trusts in You.*" *Yaytser* is the Hebrew equivalent word *mind,* meaning your "imagination."

God is so good. He says to stop thinking about those things below and start thinking about the things above (see Col. 3:2). He gave us the pattern to teach us to set our affections, our imaginations, our minds on things above, because what you behold is what you become. What you focus on, you will connect with; and when connection comes, activation takes place.

A Palace in Time

Some Jewish theologians said the Seventh Day is called a palace in time. They reasoned that it was not so much a day as an atmosphere to be experienced.

A few years ago (approximately 2004) the Lord showed me the thin veil between earth and Heaven (between this realm and the eternal). I could literally reach through this veil effortlessly and begin to interact with the realm of the spirit.

In Celtic Christian History, a term was coined to express an atmosphere where Heaven seemed so real and tangible it was as if Heaven were invading earth. The term used was "thin place"—where the fabric between the natural and spiritual realm seemed to be almost nonexistent. On this Seventh Day, we are in a "thin place" in time where the realm of the spirit is becoming much more predominant, much more real than the natural. This will become more acute and tangible to those that have eyes to see and ears to hear—those who have a passion for God and who are becoming what He says we are.

Our ability to interact with the supernatural realm will increase exponentially as this day unfolds and acceleration toward completion continues. Scripture teaches us that we as believers can be in two places simultaneously. The Word says you are already seated with Him in heavenly places (see Eph. 2:6). Since we are already seated in heavenly places in Him, why can't we interact as easily in that realm as we can in this realm? Why is it we do not see, taste, touch, smell, and hear just as easily with our spiritual senses as we do with our natural senses? According to the Word, we can—however, we have never taken the time to develop these senses to the extent as we have our natural senses.

Freedom and Rest from Work

The Seventh Day is considered a day for joy, holiness, and rest. These are all qualities of our eternal life in days to come. The words, *on the Seventh Day God finished his work*, at first looked like a puzzle (see Gen. 2:2). According to Scripture, everything He did, He did in six days. The account of Creation says that on the sixth day the Lord looked at all He had made and said that it was good—it was done (see Gen. 1:31). But it was on the Seventh Day that God finished His work. Exodus 20:11 says that in six days God made the heavens and the earth. We would think that the Bible would tell us that on the sixth day God finished His work, not on the seventh. Studying these verses, the rabbis concluded that there was actually an act of creation on the Seventh Day. They believed that on the Seventh Day God created a substance, something called "rest." What does that mean for us?

It alludes to the fact that the Lord is going to release to His people on the Seventh Day something profound, something every past generation has attempted to enter into and because of unbelief many could not. We are going to come into this place of rest. It is going to be a sovereign act of God because we are a "terminal" generation. We are the generation that will hear the Lord say, "It is finished." Every covenant promise He made is going to be fulfilled in our generation; everything He said in His Word, we are going to see come to pass. We will see the Lord Jesus descend and establish His Millennial Kingdom on this earth!

God created rest on the Seventh Day. Just as the heavens and the earth were created in six days, so rest (the Hebrew word is *menuchah*) was created on the Seventh Day. The Jewish scholars reasoned that after six days of creation, there was only one thing that the world lacked: rest. So, on the Seventh Day, when the universe and all of created matter was complete, it came to rest. All creation was in perfect symmetry and perfect harmony with no sin in it. There was no sin in it and there were no cross-purposes in it. It was in perfect harmony.

What will the realization of this rest mean for us? As we continue to purposefully and passionately pursue the Lord in this season; as we continue to grow from glory to glory, we will continue to see the Lord fuse us together with Him to such an extent that we will begin to walk in heavenly places while yet here on the earth. Our character will begin to emulate the character of Christ. Our hearts will be synchronized to that of the Father. Our actions will be motivated by love, and we will not be moved by what we see or by the tumultuous events taking place around us; for we will have learned what it truly means to "put on the Lord Jesus Christ." We will no longer make any provision for the flesh and the lusts thereof, but our hearts will be transfixed by His love.

It must and will be by grace and grace alone, lest we try to strive once again in our flesh to see the fulfillment of His promise for our lives and for this generation. It is rest; it is a fusing together of God's character with ours that is going to cause you and I to come into perfect synchronization or harmony and become one with God in thought, purpose, deed, and action. Wherever that place of rest in God is, this generation is about to experience and model it.

The Hebrew word *menuchah*, which we usually translate as "rest," means more than the cessation of labor. It means more than freedom from work or strain of any kind. *Menuchah* is considered to be something intrinsically positive. It literally means tranquility, serenity, peace, and rest. It is the state of deep peace and harmony in the soul. It is quite literally a "fusing together" of our character with God's character. It is a level of existence where no strife, no fighting, no fear, and no distress have access. It is a description of humankind at rest with God and at peace with the world in which he or she interacts.

In this place of rest, nothing will move you but God. It does not matter if all hell breaks loose around your life, you are not going to be moved. You will be at rest with God. Here is a story that a friend told me which I share mainly in other nations because they can relate to it. In Turkey some years ago there was a large textile factory that employed about 10,000 workers. There was one Christian woman who worked on the floor of this factory while the rest of the hired help was either not Christian or were Muslim. Because of her faith, this woman was subject to daily ridicule. She would continually be mocked and spit upon because she was a Christian. Her response was always to faithfully continue working at her machine and praise the Lord, saying, "Lord, thank you for the privilege of suffering for Your name's sake."

Now one day an earthquake of a magnitude of over 8.0 began to rumble and shake the factory building around her. With absolute faith in God, she lifted her hands and began to praise the Lord. The women who worked on the machines on either side of her, upon seeing her fearless response to what they believed to be the end of the world, ran to her and grabbed onto her legs and clung to her for dear life. When the earthquake ceased and the dust cleared, there were only three people left alive in that factory of 10,000—that Christian woman and the two ladies who clung to her. Now that is a picture of rest.

The rabbis believed the essence of life with God is found in the word *menuchah,* or *rest.* So much so that in later times the word became a synonym in Jewish teaching with eternal life.

In other words, the individual or group of individuals who learn what it truly means to "enter into His rest" will have a foretaste of eternal life. It is the example Moses, who was the friend of God, portrayed in his life as he was continually in the presence of the Lord and was suffused with the life essence of God. An impartation of eternal life is being released to this generation that will transform us and cause us to become everything the Word says we are. We are going to be "other" than what the Church for centuries has portrayed as Christianity. We are going to be a species set apart or as the Word says, Jew and Gentile, one new man...the essence of eternal life.

Translation by Faith

Now think about this. Moses was 120 years old and his eyes were not dim, his strength had not waned, and it says he went off into the desert and died. What he did not do was to die of any debilitating or wasting disease. I believe he received a revelation from the Lord indicating that it was time for him to go home, and so he departed into the desert and went to be with the Lord.

This generation will understand what it means to transition from this realm to the eternal realm as an act of our will. Many will hear the voice of the Lord speaking to them that it is their time to go home, and many will hear the sound of a trumpet and translate home. I firmly believe and have been hearing the Lord say there is a generation that will not taste of a physical death; there is a generation whose youth will be renewed like the eagles; there is a generation that God has raised up in this hour to walk in the full covenant promises of His Word. It is the Seventh Day, a day of completion, rest, and covenant promise fulfilled. We are that generation!

If healing is the children's bread, what happens when you mature in Christ? You don't have to get sick. You don't have to be feeble, and you don't have to walk in those things that the natural person thinks are inevitable. I don't believe in inevitability, except the inevitability of Heaven and hell. Everything, other than that, is open to the realm of faith because faith says *nothing* is impossible.

The Seventh-Day Praise

With regard to prayer, the rabbis taught that this Seventh Day is a day given to praise and worship. We have seen a tremendous increase in praise and worship throughout the nations, as with the focus of ministries being 24-hour harp and bowl—prophetic praise and proclamation. God is releasing the sounds of Heaven into the earth.

In Jewish tradition, fasting and mourning are forbidden on the Seventh Day because this day has been given by God for joy, delight, and rest. It is not the ineffective fast of Isaiah 58, where God does not hear, but it is a day of joy, delight, and rest in what God has done.

He will wipe away all tears on this day. The bride fasts until the bridegroom comes. You remember what Jesus said, "*Can the friends of the bridegroom mourn as long as the bridegroom is with them? But the days will come when the bridegroom will be taken away from them, and then they will fast*" (Matt. 9:15).

For the triumphant and overcoming believer, this day will not be a day of mourning or fasting. It will be a day of tremendous joy as the culmination of the ages comes to pass and we partake of the bounty of the Kingdom of Heaven here on earth and reap a final harvest that will be unparalleled in scope and impact.

Here we have a picture of a promise in God that points to this generation, on this Seventh Day. We would do well to set our affections and our expectations upon the Bridegroom's soon return for His bride. You have a profound destiny. You have divine purpose in God. You are part of a generation that is going to walk in realms of glory that no other generation has ever experienced or known.

Keys to the Kingdom

Last Rosh Hashanah, the Jewish New Year, I was waiting on the Lord and seeking His face. This has been my practice during the season of September/October because for the last six or seven years I have had an encounter with the Lord on this day. On this particular Rosh Hashanah, the Lord began by showing me what looked like a very large skeleton key. As I was watching and waiting for the Lord to explain to me what He was trying to convey, all of a sudden this key began to grow, and I thought, *Oh my goodness, it is going to explode!* At that moment, I sensed the heart of the Father and there was a tangible excitement in His heart, and He began to speak to me, "I'm releasing keys, the keys I have given to the Church, and in this season they are pregnant with possibility."

I immediately understood that we are on the threshold of some of the most profound displays of His miracle-working power that I believe the world has ever seen. I knew in my spirit that the Father had been awaiting and anticipating this fullness-of-time season in which He was going to release these attesting miracles in the earth because they are to be a part of the last great move of God.

You are His inheritance and you are Christ's inheritance. You are the bride that He has prepared for His Son. He is excited. He is about to say "Son, go get her!" The Father is excited right now because He is about to release to this generation, to this Church, an understanding of the keys of the Kingdom that have been impregnated with possibility for this generation.

In another season of fasting and prayer, this time over New Years 2008, the Lord spoke and said, "There will be an explosion of My glory beginning this year!" During that year, the Lord began to move spontaneously in various nations of the world as He gave us a glimpse of what He has in store in greater measure in the coming days. What we have seen and experienced is only the birth-pang of what we are about to be engulfed by.

Let me give you just a small glimpse of some of what the Lord has been showing me. The time is at hand that when a friend or acquaintance asks you a simple question such as, "What have you been up to?" or "Where did you go today?" you will be able to say, "I went to paradise, and I talked with Abraham for a while." Or your answer will be, "I've visited three nations and ministered to a number of people as the Lord directed." How is this going to be possible? I have personally experienced translation on a number of occasions, and I've met others whom the Lord has supernaturally translated to different geographic locations in order to serve His purposes. We are entering a season where, for the Christian, this will become more of the norm than the exception.

We are literally a people of two realms! We are going to be a people that will begin to interact with the Lord in ways that some of the saints' past generations interacted with Him. Study Church history. You will find amazing historical testimony of some astounding miracles in the lives of saints of old.

Throughout history, we have seen men and women, a select few, who were passionate in their pursuit of God in their generation. They became shining pillars to their respective generations— testifying by their lives and actions to the possibility of God. In this day, we are about to see a whole Body of believers who in their passionate pursuit of the Lord are going to connect with God and transform this world. A harvest is taking place. It is time for us to stand as soldiers of the King, fully vested with the authority of God, unflinchingly donning the armor of God and boldly proclaiming the Word of God!

> Father, I thank you for your love and for the great privilege of being a group of hand selected men and women called to a great destiny on this day. There has never been a day like this before, nor shall there be any like it afterward. Lord, we are so privileged and honored, even though you are only giving us a glimpse, God, because we can't comprehend the whole. Father, the glimpse that

you've given us is overwhelming. This is a prophetic season unlike any other season in the history of this planet. Father I pray that the seeds that we just released into your people will increase quickly and Father, that they will bring forth fruit a hundred-fold. Water that word Father. Water the revelation that was from your heart. Lord, by your grace, help us to enter into your rest through obedience to your Word. In Jesus' mighty name, amen.

ENDNOTE

1. S. Ferguson, D. Wright, J. I. Packer, eds. *New International Dictionary of New Testament Theology,* Vol. 3 (Downers Grove, IL: Intervarsity Press, 1988).

CHAPTER 4

Obedience and Passion

I n the last chapter we looked at what some of what the ancient rabbis had passed down as traditional thought throughout their generations. The possibility of God in this season is unparalleled in all of history.

In Exodus 13:3-10, *Moses said to the people: "Remember this day in which you went out of Egypt, out of the house of bondage; for by strength of hand the Lord brought you out of this place. No leaven bread shall be eaten. On this day you are going out, in the month Abib. And it shall be, when the Lord brings you into the land of the Canaanites and the Hittites and the Amorites and the Hivites and the Jebusites, which He swore to your fathers to give you a land flowing with milk and honey, that you shall keep this service in this month. Seven days you shall eat unleavened bread, and on the seventh day there shall be a feast to the Lord. Unleavened bread shall be eaten seven days. And no leavened bread shall be seen among you, nor shall leaven be seen among you in all your quarters. And you shall tell your son in that day, saying, 'This is done because of what the Lord did for me when I came up from Egypt'. It shall be as a sign to you on your hand and as a memorial between your eyes that the Lords law may be in your mouth; for with a strong hand the Lord has brought you out of Egypt. You shall therefore keep this ordinance in its season from year to year.'"*

The Lord is speaking to us in a very significant way on this Seventh Day. As I said earlier, everything we see in the Word regarding the Seventh Day points to a specific prophetic time in history. As stated in Chapter 2, the Law of First Mention is a valid tool that God gave us to study the Scriptures. Once again, that Law of First Mention is simply stated as this: "The first time something is mentioned in Scripture, in context, from that point on, you can use this *first mention* as a basis to interpret all other Scriptures that speak of the same subject."

Let's do a quick review: the very first time we heard of the Seventh Day was when God finished all that He began and He rested. He called that Seventh Day holy. It was sanctified and set apart. It has a profound significance and purpose, and it speaks of a generation of destiny that shall come forth at the time of the end. This day has the heart and the fingerprint of the Father all over it. God instituted an ordinance that Israel would remember the Seventh Day every week as a memorial to remember what God had done in their lives and how He had brought them out of Egypt. Now Egypt, allegorically speaking, is a type and shadow of the world.

When we get together on the Seventh Day, we are adhering to a covenant of remembrance established by the Lord. Not only does it require us to reflect and be thankful, but this day also served the purpose of prophetically pointing to a day in the future when God would complete all that He began. This remembrance pointed to a specific thousand-year day—a millennium, the Seventh Day, when the Lord will bring all of His creation into rest. All will be completed and every covenant promise will be fulfilled.

We are transitioning from one form of government to the government of Jesus our King who is soon to establish His earthly Kingdom to rule and reign for a thousand years.

Overcoming Giants

Let me give you some definitions that will help you to better understand some of the *giants* in our corporate and individual promised lands that hinder us from our rightful possession of what God has promised us:

The Canaanites—means possessor or purchaser

The Hittites—means one who is broken, or one who fears

The Amorites—means bitter, a rebel, or a babbler

The Hivites—means wicked, refers to wickedness

The Jebusites—means one trodden underfoot; to be polluted or unclean.

Canaanites

Each of us faces Canaanites—the temptation of selling our birthright by taking the less difficult path or the path of least resistance. Compromise is rampant within the Church community. In an attempt to appease the world and not be offensive, the Church has relegated the truth of God's Word and will to an intellectual assent open to debate and the mores of current society. Jesus faced this same temptation twice in His earthly ministry. Early on during His temptation in the wilderness, He was offered everything that was rightfully His, if He would only bow His knee to the usurper, satan. He would not need to struggle and suffer if He would only acquiesce to the less noble path of compromise. His response was in all points the upraised standard of God's Word.

His second test came in the Garden of Gethsemane when the battle raged around Him to finish the course set before Him. The struggle was so severe and the temptation so powerful that He sweat great drops of blood. His response models for us the necessary heart attitude required to overcome the first of the squatters in our promised land; *"He went a little farther and fell on His face, and prayed, saying, "O My Father, if it is possible, let this cup pass from Me; nevertheless, not as I will, but as You will"* (Matt. 26:39).

Hittites

The second challenge we will face as we continue toward possession of our promised land is overcoming the Hittites—one who is broken or one who fears. There is a brokenness that will lead to repentance, and it will open the door to the transformation of our inner man allowing the Lord to perfect His character within us.

> *The sacrifices of God are a broken spirit, a broken and a contrite heart—these, O God, You will not despise* (Psalm 51:17).

There is also a brokenness that opens the door to condemnation, which causes us to walk in fear. Fear is the antithesis of faith—the exact opposite of faith. It will paralyze an individual and cause flight rather than fight! The solution to a spirit of fear is perfect love shed abroad in our hearts because perfect love casts out all fear (see 1 John 4:18). Carnal fear comes through a lack of faith. The solution to that type of fear is spending time in the Word of God (see Rom. 10:17).

Amorites

Our third contest will come in the guise of the Amorite—bitterness. It is striking the amount of anger and bitterness that is prevalent within the Church community. I firmly believe that the most subtle of our enemies and the one that takes more people captive is this particular snare. We justify our actions and our reactions to individuals brashly stating our right to be angry and retaliate in direct contradiction to God's Word. Unaddressed bitterness in the life of the believer will open the door to much of the curse from which we were released with the shed blood of Christ. Yet, if we do not avail ourselves of this precious gift through repentance and forgiveness, we will be consumed by our individual Amorites. Many Scriptures deal specifically with this issue, so I will only name a few:

> *For if you forgive men their trespasses, your heavenly Father will also forgive you* (Matthew 6:14).

> *Then Peter came to Him and said, "Lord, how often shall my brother sin against me, and I forgive him? Up to seven times?" Jesus said to him, "I do not say to you, up to seven times, but up to seventy times seven* (Matthew 18:21-22).

> *Let all bitterness, wrath, anger, clamor, and evil speaking be put away from you, with all malice. And be kind to one another, tenderhearted, forgiving one another, even as God in Christ forgave you* (Ephesians 4:31-32).

Hivites

The Hivites—or wickedness—pose our fourth challenge to possessing our promised land on this Seventh Day. Wickedness begins in the heart of humans and germinates until it is released in full bloom. It was because of wickedness that the Lord became grieved in His heart and repented that He had even made man (see Gen. 6:5-6). We find a principle woven throughout Scripture that, in effect, says that what we focus on we will become. When we allow our minds, our thoughts, to continually meditate or think upon unrighteousness, we begin to become hardened to the sensory stimuli that inundates us on a regular basis and eventually leads us to compromise in our Christian walk.

Let me give you an example. My wife, Reshma, is from a very conservative East Indian family in Fiji. She was raised in an atmosphere with a standard of conduct that would not make room for worldly influences that most of us no longer even notice. Anything that was considered contrary to the standard of purity required for a believer in God's Word was not allowed in the home. Whether that was a particular television show that had questionable content or personal conduct outside of the home with friends, conduct unbecoming of a set-apart child of God was not sanctioned or allowed.

Now fast forward to when I brought her to America for the first time with our loose moral conduct, our acceptance of unbiblical types of behavior, our loose language, and lack of respect for our elders as well as our disrespect of the Word of God in many venues. To say that she was shocked is the understatement of the century! What I had become hardened to because of my proximity and emersion into this culture was appalling to someone who had lived a life of separation unto God. Wickedness no longer grieved me, because I lived in a society that had lost its sensitivity to holiness, purity, and the fear of God. The Scripture refers to it in this way:

> *And delivered righteous Lot, who was oppressed by the filthy conduct of the wicked (for that righteous man, dwelling among them, tormented his righteous soul from day to day by seeing and hearing their lawless deeds)* (2 Peter 2:7-8).

It is through seeing and hearing that we become inured to unrighteousness around us. We must, as David did, make a covenant with our eyes not even to look upon that which God considers wicked or evil. We must protect our ears and keep ourselves from listening to unrighteousness. We must sensitize ourselves to the heart of the Father and to the still small voice of the Holy Spirit. Only in this way will we guard ourselves from the influence of the

Hivites in our promised land. And once we know how to guard ourselves from their influence, we are armed and ready to destroy their influence wherever we go.

Jebusites

Our final contest is with the Jebusites—to be polluted or unclean. Pollution comes through conformity to the societal mores allowing them to take precedence over God's Word. Conformity literally comes through compromise. Compromise comes because we either do not know or we will not adhere to the principles of God's Word.

> *Do not be conformed to this world (this age), [fashioned after and adapted to its external, superficial customs], but be transformed (changed) by the [entire] renewal of your mind [by its new ideals and its new attitude], so that you may prove [for yourselves] what is the good and acceptable and perfect will of God, even the thing which is good and acceptable and perfect [in His sight for you]* (Romans 12:2 AMP).

Compromise will also position us for defeat in every area of our lives. We will literally be trodden down of the enemy and overcome if we allow the Jebusites to go uncontested in our journey into this Seventh Day and our promised land.

Spiritual Warfare

All of the things in the "Promised Land" that God says belong to us on this Seventh Day are received by faith and a genuine recognition of our need to be holy before Him. We created a false expectation in the Church that portrays the "true" Christian life as a life that will be free of stress, hardship, and the challenge of everyday mundane life. This is a distorted and unrealistic view. The reality is, when we begin to possess our promised land, the battle begins! Thank

God, the Lord has restored to the Church an understanding of spiritual warfare. Yet I believe we are entering into a season of greater understanding than ever before regarding what spiritual warfare is, and in the midst of our challenges, the Lord is beginning to release new strategies and new revelation on how to take our promised land.

Spiritual warfare simply stated is this: walking in discernment and doing what the Lord tells you to do—nothing more and nothing less. Spiritual warfare is obedience to God. We have seen all types of programs established as a means to bring victory in spiritual warfare, and some of them even worked! Our society has cultivated the mind-set that thinks the more involved and intellectual the approach is to any type of challenge, be they natural or spiritual, the more effective the results will be. We've seen (and tried to use) the three-step programs on how to get someone delivered. Then we had to have a ten-step program on how to keep them delivered, as well as instituting a program and an ongoing discussion of both the effectiveness and practicality of the three-step program and the ten-step program! On top of that was the 47-step program on how to maintain both the three-step and the ten-step programs!

I am taking this to an extreme to highlight the glaring need for new strategies from Heaven for this day; a day of *rest*—a ceasing from our own works, as God did from His. Programs, while they helped to restore an awareness of the fact that we are in a spiritual battle, are no substitute for being led by the Spirit of God. New strategies are being released for this new day, and we must embrace the new wineskin if we are going to be effective in walking in Kingdom authority in this hour. New strategies are received as we learn to wait upon the Lord to receive our daily marching orders.

For some in the Church, this terrifies them because they really have never developed a real sensitivity to the voice of God and so they flounder in their Christian walk. I've asked this question all over the world: "How many of you hear the voice of God on a regular basis?" In a room full of 200 or 300 people, only two or three hands go up. The problem is, if you do not hear the voice of God, you cannot be saved!

Recognizing the Voice of God

Somehow, once we get saved, we subscribe to the notion that the Lord only speaks through His Word. While it is true that the foundation and plumb-line of all that the Lord speaks is His Word, His voice is much more than that. If you can remember when you first began to recognize the wooing of the Holy Spirit in your life, you will understand better what the voice of God encompasses: there was a drawing, there was a conviction, there was an unction, an overwhelming emotion. There might have been visions, and there might have been an audible voice. His Word may have impacted you; revelation broke forth in your heart, and you knew the reality of God in that moment. In all of these examples, we see facets of the voice of God at work in communicating with us. So why is it that once we become Christians we limit the Lord to words only? Have you ever heard the expression, *A picture paints a thousand words*? At its most basic, visions are the voice of God in a form we do not usually equate to language.

So many ask the question, "How do I hear God's voice?" My answer is, "How do you not hear God's voice?" Everything God does speaks! His name is *The Word!* He speaks. You can't find one vision in the Bible that wasn't the voice of God speaking. The means of communication in Heaven is vastly different than the means by which we communicate here on earth. The most ineffective form of communication is verbal! Every one of us has had the experience of saying one thing, and the person you were talking to heard something exactly opposite of what you said.

On a number of occasions, while having a vision of Heaven or actually being there (see 2 Cor. 12:1-3), I have experienced what communication is like in that realm. Communication is instantaneous and it is heart to heart and mind to mind. There will be absolutely no confusion; nor will there be any misunderstanding of what was communicated. The closest we come to that here on earth is when we receive words of knowledge, words of wisdom, or prophecy. It is an instant download of insight and understanding.

Power to Reach the Promise

The transition from the sixth day to the Seventh Day is fraught with potential pitfalls. We have before us the greatest opportunity of any generation that has preceded us, and yet we are in the greatest danger of missing this auspicious moment. There *are* giants in the land. This means there are victories to be won and there are enemies to be defeated. We will not, however, persevere by adhering to yesterday's strategies; nor will we be victorious by embracing the antiquated religious system of past generations. We cannot continue to allow a mixture of flesh and unsanctified reasoning to lead us. We must allow the Word to pierce us deeply in this tumultuous time and choose to be conformed to His image. We must put on the mind of Christ and we must protect ourselves against the insidious lure of a lukewarm gospel that appears to be righteous and holy but is devoid of power or presence. Those who choose to embrace the cross in our generation will not tolerate mixture, and the Lord will release them to the promise of this Seventh Day.

What comes to mind when we speak of the Promised Land? According to Scripture, the Promised Land carries with it the full acceptance, entrance into, and access to all of the benefits of the covenant of God being released and realized in our lives. It indicates intimacy with God. My Promised Land is realized when my relationship with the Lord becomes so intimate that there is a fusion of my being together with His to such an extent that my character and all of its defects are transformed into His character; the motives of my heart are purified and are completely given over and aligned with Him. As I enter into this Promised Land, I become the richest man on earth! Partaking of His nature and His character will open the door to a realm of living and moving and having my being in a way that very few have ever experienced (see Acts 17:28). This is exactly what lies before us during this season of rest and completion. This is the promise of the Seventh Day!

The Feast of the Lord

Another significant event that is to shortly take place on the Seventh Day is there will be a feast to the Lord, a holy convocation. It is called the marriage supper of the Lamb (see Rev. 19:7). Many are invited to this feast, and yet the response has been less than stellar (see Matt. 22:2-14).

A few years ago I had an experience where I was caught up into the third heaven, and the first person I met displayed great excitement because of the anticipation and preparation taking place for a great banquet. She said, "Bruce, it's so exciting! We are seeing so much activity, and preparations are nearly complete!" When I inquired what this banquet was for she responded, "The marriage supper of the Lamb is about to take place."

She then went on to say, "So many people are visiting Heaven and returning to earth to proclaim that all is ready and to invite those called to attend to be prepared."

According to Jewish tradition, the rabbis ruled that the Sabbath (Seventh Day) should be made the specific object of honor (*kavod*) and delight (*oneg*), based on the verse in Isaiah 58:13, *If you call the Sabbath a delight, the holy day of the Lord honorable.* Traditionally, "honor" implied the duties of bathing immediately before the Sabbath, wearing special Sabbath clothes, and receiving the Sabbath with joy.

> *He shall purify himself with the water on the third day and on the **seventh day**; then he will be clean. But if he does not purify himself on the third day and on the seventh day, he will not be clean* (Numbers 19:12).

> *The clean person shall sprinkle the unclean on the third day and on the seventh day; and on the **seventh day** he shall purify himself, wash his clothes, and bathe in water; and at evening he shall be clean* (Numbers 19:19).

The washing of the water of the Word as well as the continual application of the blood of Jesus are prerequisites for the Seventh Day. The compelling weight of Scripture continually tells us to be a people of the Word. The washing of the water of the Word is not only our birth right but is necessary for continued growth and health within the Kingdom of God. A heart that is quick to repent at the slightest conviction of the Holy Spirit is almost a foreign concept in many movements today that espouse a gospel devoid of power or consequence.

Delighting in the Sabbath

Delight meant lighting candles on Friday night (as the Sabbath began), enjoying special delicacies, eating a minimum of three Sabbath meals, cohabiting with one's spouse, and engaging in general repose (rest) and added sleep.[2]

The prophetic symbolism of our "delighting" in the Sabbath is very telling. Without having to write another book, let me give you just a sampling of the symbolism inherent in these observances. The parable of the ten virgins is the first depiction of a New Testament example that comes to mind (see Matt. 25:1-10). The enjoyment of special delicacies refers to a palate that is capable of discerning and enjoying the choicest of the meats offered (see Heb. 5:14). Cohabiting with our spouse depicts an intimacy with the Bridegroom for this generation that is beyond our ability to fully grasp. Three Sabbath meals with one's spouse (we are the bride of Christ), speaks of an intimate sharing of the bread of the Word, all while at rest.

Traditionally, the woman of the house would light at least two candles on Friday evening (again, the parable of the ten virgins in Matthew 25) corresponding to the two ways in which the Fourth Commandment is phrased—"remember" (Exod. 20:8) and "observe" (Deut. 5:12) the Sabbath day. These two candles also symbolized the unity underlying all apparent duality: man and woman, body and soul, speech and silence, Creation and Revelation.

Additionally, in order not to desecrate the Sabbath by miscalculating the precise time that night falls and the Seventh Day begins, it is customary to light the candles 18 minutes before sunset on Friday evening.

In the study of biblical numerology, the number 18 refers to judgment, rebellion, defection, corruption, and disintegration. It is interesting to me that as we enter into this Seventh Day, we as believers are told the glory of the Lord would arise upon us as when wickedness and gross darkness are in the ascendancy in this world at the end of the age (see Isa. 60:2).

The moment at which the Sabbath candles are lit is considered a favorable time for God to hear the woman's (the bride's) personal prayer. Believe me when I tell you, all of Heaven is watching and listening as these final moments of history unfold!

This is just a sampling of the prophetic insight that is available to us that helps to define what this Seventh Day entails.

Many are having visions and experiences in the third heaven as a sign to this generation of the impending return of the Lord. Visitations of angels and even visitations by Jesus are being reported in almost every nation with the same recurring theme: He's coming sooner than most people think.

The Lord is preparing a feast where unleavened bread shall be eaten for seven days. In a conversation with the Lord during my time of worship and study, I said "Lord, I know You said beware of the leaven of the Pharisees. What exactly is that? Tradition? Looking good in the eyes of men and women? False teaching?" Immediately, the Spirit said this, "When the marriage supper of the Lamb takes place, the bride will be caught away, and those who remain will have seven more years of tribulation before I come to establish My Kingdom." The eternal destination of those who remain will be determined upon whether or not they partake of the leaven of this modern-day religious system that proclaims false doctrine and leads men to destruction.

Beware of False Doctrines

We must be a people who adhere to the biblical admonition of being separated unto God. We must choose to spend as much time as possible in the Word of God, rightly dividing the Word of truth, so there will be no leaven that causes us to follow tradition and doctrines contrary to Scripture. Even now, there are doctrines of demons in mainline churches as well as in charismatic churches that are being portrayed and perpetrated as truth according to Scripture. If we do not know God's Word, then we will buy into these deceptions without hesitation.

Jesus said it is possible that even the very elect will be deceived if He didn't shorten the days (see Matt. 24:22). None are exempt from the possibility of deception ensnaring us. We need to be aware of this danger and prepare as much as is possible by urgently pressing into God. I am not advocating an attitude of fear and doubt or wondering whether you are out of step with the Lord and His Word, not at all. Trust your Father in Heaven—that He sees your heart and He sees that you want to walk with Him in truth. Then He will bring you into truth. Don't accept everything you hear being taught from pulpits as truth. Don't even accept everything I am teaching without going to the Word and finding out the truth for yourself. Be a student of the Word—study to show yourself approved unto God (see 2 Tim. 2:15). If what is taught cannot stand the scrutiny of Scripture, it is not from God.

Exodus 13:7 says, *"No leavened bread shall be seen among you, nor shall any leaven be seen among you in all your quarters."* In other words, nothing you do, nothing you touch, nothing you eat, nothing you behold, nothing you listen to; in all aspects of your life, do not let any leaven cause the truth of God's Word to be substituted by the traditions of humankind or doctrines based on a religious system of indoctrination. Instead, get hold of truth, get hold of life, get hold of what God is saying and cling to it.

As a nation, we have the largest smorgasbord of Christian material of any nation on earth available to us, but according to what I have seen and experienced in the many nations I have traveled to, we seem to have the most lukewarm Church of any nation we've been to! Because of the availability of the tools so readily at hand, we take for granted the privilege set before us of using these resources to grow in Christ and gain a greater understanding and a greater intimacy with Him.

The Key of Passion

As I've studied the Bible, I have found a major, if not *the* major key, in growing in knowledge and intimacy with the Lord. It is the key of passion! A desperate hunger will cause an individual to take desperate measures to satisfy that hunger! If you have an abundance of everything and you've never known hunger, you become ambivalent; you become lackluster in your approach to the study of God's Word, and undecided about the truth of that Word because you've never had to prove the reality of His Word in your everyday existence. If I'd never had to stand on Scripture as my only option, I would have never come to understand the power of that Word.

It has been passion and hunger—desperation for God—that motivated saints of old to obtain the promises of God for their lives. You find this key at work from Genesis to Revelation. A zeal for God, a fervor for Jesus, a passion for truth, always arrests the attention of Heaven and leads you to the truth. His name is Jesus. If you do not have passion for this journey that God has given, you won't go very far, and you will get there quick.

From the first day I received Jesus into my heart I've had a burning passion to know Him more. I do not fully know why the Lord gave me passion in my life. I do know it is the grace of God at work. I am grateful, and because of this deep hunger I have never been satisfied with where I am at in Christ. I am just *not* satisfied. The more I taste of God, the hungrier I get. It has felt to me as if the more I learn the less I know and the greater the hunger becomes to discover Him.

I have had a number of visions and visitations from the Lord, and as grateful as I am for all that He has blessed me with, I am not satisfied! These experiences have made me hungry for more. I hear of the experiences that other people have, and I hunger! I have become the epitome of a starving, desperate individual who can *never* get enough. I want it all! I am greedy for God! Jeremiah 29:11-13 says you can have all of Him you want, and I'm determined to passionately pursue Him for all that He is.

With a strong hand, the Lord has brought us out of Egypt (see Exod. 13:3). With a strong hand! With a strong hand the Lord on *this* Seventh Day is going to do something: He is going to take Egypt out of us and He is going to take us out of this world! He is going to remove every hindrance, every obstacle, every blockade that has kept us from our destiny and the promise of God that says on this day of completion we will be complete in Him, not just figuratively but in actuality. We will experience the fulfillment of every covenant promise in our generation! The key for us in this hour is *passion*! Do not be found to be the lukewarm Church on this day! Fan the flame of passion in your heart—return to your first love and allow Jesus to become your magnificent obsession in this hour once again!

You do not have to figure out how to go from where you are to passion. You do not have to try and work out a discipline to get you there. You just have to say, "Yes, Lord!" You see, God put you here on this earth for a purpose in this generation. You have a remarkable destiny as a child of God in the generation. This season is one of the most extraordinary seasons that we believers will ever experience.

No Limits in God

One expression being bantered about in Christian circles of those walking in a realm of revelation that has not been experienced before, refers to them as being "on the cutting edge." While that has some merit to it, my heart is to be beyond the cutting edge! My heart's desire and my passion lead me to believe there are no limits in God for those who believe! For too long, we have settled for far less than has been available to us, and while I have been grateful for all those who have been on the *cutting edge*, I long for more. I want to be so far out there, I don't even see the cutting edge. I am believing for things I've never seen and things I've never heard!

If we will use what we have—our heartfelt resounding cry of "yes Lord," then the Lord will meet us there and will make up the deficit in our lives. At that point, we will enter into our destiny and our faith will increase.

> *Then Moses spoke to Aaron, "...all the congregation of the children of Israel, 'Come near before the Lord, for He has heard your complaints.'" Now it came to pass, as Aaron spoke to the whole Congregation of the children of Israel, that they looked toward the wilderness, and behold, the glory of the Lord appeared in the cloud* (Exodus 16:9-10).

As Christians, our natural proclivity is to avoid, at all costs, any wilderness experience we can. Yet, that is where the glory of God is experienced and recognized for what it is! The example of Jesus' life shows us that He frequently went into the wilderness to be alone with the Father. It was a place of intimate communion with the Lord, not just a place of test and temptation.

Exodus 16:11-12 continues: *The Lord spoke to Moses saying, "I have heard the complaints of the children of Israel. Speak to them, saying, 'At twilight you shall eat meat, and in the morning, you shall be filled with bread. And you shall know that I am Lord your God....'"*

Then verse 22 says, *"And so it was, on the sixth day, that they gathered twice as much bread, two omers for each one. And all the rulers of the congregation came and told Moses* (Exodus 16:22).

Now we know *six* is the number of man. For six days, the Lord gave stewardship of this vineyard to men. For six days, by the sweat of the brow or our intellectual understanding, we have gathered bread. But now we are in transition from the sixth day to the Seventh Day, and something supernatural is happening. We are entering a day (the Seventh) that requires from us a new strategy; a concept that is foreign to our way of thinking and doing.

The Pouring out of New Manna

We must understand that our striving and intellectualizing will be fruitless in this hour. If we try to utilize and consume yesterday's manna (the revelation released for past moves of God) in this new season, it will become putrid and disgusting upon our tongues. It is full of worms! We need new manna today, and it will be a double portion. As we transition into the Seventh Day, we will experience a release of the *double portion* that will sustain us and enable us for the day(s) ahead.

During this season of transition, the Lord is releasing extraordinary insight and revelation, a double portion that will allow us to enter into and remain at rest. In John chapter 2 we read the story of the wedding feast in Cana which took place on the third day (remember we are also actively transitioning from the second day into the third day). (See John 2:1-12.) When there was no longer any wine, His mother told the servants to do whatever He told them to do. Jesus told them to fill six water pots with water, to draw forth the water and to give it to the master of the feast. It was while drawing forth the water and giving it to the master of the feast that it became new wine.

As we draw from the deposit of the water of the Word, in our hearts, a transformation takes place and new wine is released. In other words, as we sow what we have of the Word, new revelation comes forth for a new day! We are seeing a release of fresh manna, a double portion's worth in this hour. It is revelation reserved for this generation that will release us into the fullness of the stature of the knowledge of God.

It seems I cannot pick up the Bible anymore without an outpouring of fresh revelation. There were seasons in my life where I would read and study the Bible and it was like being lost in space. Now, I am almost overwhelmed as I pick up the Word and begin to read.

> *He said to them, 'Tomorrow is a Sabbath rest, a Holy Sabbath to the Lord, bake what you will bake today, and boil what you will boil; and lay out for yourselves all that remains, to be kept until morning'* (Exodus 16:23).

Interestingly enough, earlier in verse 12, it says "*You will have meat in the evening*" (see Exod. 16:12). Now according to the Jewish understanding, the Sabbath begins on Friday evening. It was during the transition from one day to the other, at sunset, that the new day began. We are just entering into our Sabbath day, the Seventh Day. The transition is underway, and it is time for the meat! Strong meat belongs to those who "*by reason of use have their senses exercised to discern both good and evil*" (Heb. 5:14). We are coming of age on this day and we will be able to rightly divide the Word of truth. Maturity will be realized by many of God's people on this day. Exodus 16:24-26 says,

> *So they [saved] it…till morning, as Moses commanded; and it did not stink, nor were there any worms in it. Then Moses said, "Eat that today, for today is a Sabbath to the Lord; today you will not find it in the field. Six days you shall gather it, but on the seventh day, the Sabbath, there will be none.*

Neither the arm of flesh, the reasoning of men and women, nor theology, doctrine, nor traditions, are going to feed your spirit-man anymore. You have to get manna from Heaven, and it has to be fresh and new.

Divine Guidance From Heaven

There are resources in Heaven that God has reserved for this generation and this generation alone. The manna sustained them for 40 years in the wilderness and the manna we are going to partake of in this generation will prepare us for eternity. Multitudes are going to have a taste, a glimpse, and an experience with eternal things as the Lord releases to us the promise of the Seventh Day. There are indicators and signs all over the earth of this heavenly invasion. Two of our friends, Harold (who has since gone Home to be with the Lord) and Kaye Bayer, would literally and supernaturally receive manna from Heaven. This manifestation occurred for over 30 years in their ministry and travels. When shared with individuals around the world, many were healed and set free. This is a clear sign of God's provision for His children.

> Exodus 16:27-28 says, *Now it happened that some of the people went out on the seventh day to gather, but they found none. And the Lord said to Moses, "How long [will] you refuse to keep my commandments and my laws?"*

The Lord watches those He puts in the position of leadership and authority. Five-fold ministry is to prepare you for what God called you to do. (See Ephesians 4:11.) If the ministry cannot get you eating fresh manna and beginning to chew the meat, if they cannot connect you with what God says is your destiny in this day, they have failed. It is not about coming to hear a wonderful sermon and being entertained every week. It is about seeing your life changed and seeing you become all that you are called to be and then releasing you to function in your God-given purpose. Once again, we are reminded in the above verses that yesterday's methods will not work today. The *programs* of the past will not have the ability any longer to nourish and sustain a Church that is called to be hidden away in Him and sustained solely by Him. Even if we search for those old methods, they will no longer be found by us.

Exodus 16:29-30 says, *For the Lord has given you the Sabbath, therefore He gives you on the Sixth day bread for two days. Let every man remain in his place; let no man go out of his place on the seventh day [the Sabbath]. So the people rested....*

This is powerful. Our place is to be found in *Him*. We are His Body. We are to remain in Him and no longer be moved by our own motivations, but to move only when He moves and to go only where He goes. The book of Joel speaks of an army that's going to come forth at the end of the age. Joel 2:7 speaks about everyone marching within their ranks, and they do not move out of their place. They only move as one when God speaks. That is the picture of *rest* during the end of the age. When this army moves, the enemy flees because we are now in unison; the Body has become one living organism, acting in perfect harmony and symmetry.

We have got to be people who partake of the manna and eat of the meat, a people who get into our place and remain in our place. We must only move when He says move and only speak when He says speak, and only do what He tells us to do. Then, the Canaanites, the Hivites, the Jebusites, and the Amorites are going to be eradicated, and all that will be left are the "favor-ites." That is us!

Exodus 20:8 says, *Remember the Sabbath day, to keep it holy.*

Keep this in the forefront of your heart. Let it resonate within your spirit! Write it on your walls if you have to, but understand: This day is holy to God! This Seventh Day is sanctified and set apart with purpose for God. It has been anticipated by the Father for 6,000 years or six days. He has looked forward to this generation. With great anticipation Jesus has been looking forward to this season and this time because the Father is about to say, "Go get Your Bride! Go, bring her home!"

Six days you shall labor and do all your work, but the Seventh Day is the Sabbath of the Lord your God; in it, you shall do *no* work! We must stop using the arm of flesh to accomplish the purposes of God! Please, hear my heart when I say this: everywhere I go, well-meaning people say, "We know the ministry can't go forward without finances." While we acknowledge an element of truth to that statement, we must recognize that we are limiting God by speaking such things. The Gospel *can* be preached without finances. The Gospel is not restricted by humankind's economy! The Lord will get the job done, even if He has to provide ravens to feed you or supply manna from Heaven for you, or feed you with honey out of a dead lion. The Lord can and will get the job done. We have to re-think some of our unscriptural stances and learn to rely on the Lord in *all* things, not just those things we seemingly have no control over. The resources of Heaven are vast and limitless.

Miracle in Malaysia

We know a pastor in Kuala Lumpur, Malaysia who shared with us an amazing testimony about the Lord's ability to miraculously supply needed resources. In the early days of their ministry, they were in a house they had rented for their church, and the Lord said, "Believe for a church building." So they began to exercise their faith and believe God for a particular building that was for sale across the street from where they were, at that time, meeting. The church consisted of approximately 20 people in the congregation. The pastor, after investigating the building and agreeing to purchase it for a specified sum of money, told his congregation they would need about 75,000 ringgit to close the deal (the currency of Malaysia is the Ringgit. It is about 1/3 the value of US $1.00).

During that time, the offerings in the Church were not much, as the average income was very low. The pastor's faith was such, however, that he was unshakeable in his stance and belief that he had heard from the Lord and that the Lord would provide.

The Sunday before they were to go to the real estate office (they were to be there on Monday morning, the very next day) he stood in his pulpit before the receiving of the offering and stated that God was not a liar. The Lord had told them the building was theirs and so there would be enough to purchase the building!

As they were receiving the offering, the pastor stood and watched as the offering bag was being passed. What he saw with his natural eye was very few ringgit going into the offering bag. When everyone had an opportunity to give, the pastor said, "Bring the offering up here; we are going to count it."

While standing at the pulpit, they reached into the offering bag and began pulling out money, time after time after time, they continued to reach into that bag until they had counted 78 *thousand* ringgit! The Lord had performed a creative miracle of multiplication with that currency until there was enough for the purchase of their new building!

What blessed me was he wasn't even surprised at the Lord's ability to provide in such a way! What did surprise him was the amount. As far as he understood, the church only needed 75,000 ringgit. The next day when they went down to the office to make the purchase of the building and sign the papers, they found there was another 3,000 ringgit of unexpected filing fees they hadn't been told about. The Lord knew in advance exactly how much was needed, and He provided exceedingly, abundantly above what they had asked or even considered (see Eph. 3:20). God is not affected by the economy of this earth.

We limit God with tradition and our natural reasoning. We must discover that once we accepted Christ, we became new creatures. We are supernatural beings, and we have a supernatural God. We must stop limiting ourselves to the limitations of the natural realm. We serve a supernatural God, and we are supernatural beings. All things are possible to him that believes (see Mark 9:23).

ENDNOTES

1. Hitchcock's Bible Names Dictionary, http://www.ccel.org/ccel/hitchcock/bible_names.tp.html.

2. Ronald Eisenberg, *JPS Guide to Jewish Traditions* (Philadelphia, PA: The Jewish Publications Society, 2004).

CHAPTER 5

The Sign of the Sabbath

And the Lord spoke to Moses, saying, "Speak also to the children of Israel, saying, 'surely My Sabbaths you shall keep, for it is a sign…'" (Exodus 31:12-13).

T he Seventh Day was to be for a sign and a remembrance of all the Lord had done for His covenant people as well as a sign of the covenant He has with His people. It was intended to cause the nation of Israel to remember the promises of God and to reflect upon the fulfillment of those promises. It was a prototype pointing to a certain day—a day of fulfillment. It is a day of completion and rest and it pointed to this day.

This Seventh Day is to be the day of fulfillment that the previous archetype pointed to. During this new day, we will be witness to some of the most unusual signs and wonders and attesting miracles ever displayed before in recorded human history. These will be released through us, as well as sovereignly rain down upon us. *This* Seventh Day is a sign and it will be full of supernatural manifestations that defy the natural mind.

The Day of Sanctification

The Seventh Day was also a day of sanctification. There will be a completion of the process of sanctification for those who are embracing the promise this day holds. The Lord will complete that which He began in us. He is going to bring us to the place of consecration, separation, and sanctification that belongs to us. We are going to be what He says we are.

From the age of 14, when I accepted Christ, I would pursue God after a fashion that was modeled for me in a religious setting. The truth was that I really wanted God, but I didn't know how to reach Him. I would say, "God, I want to be sanctified, I want to be what You want me to be!" I would pursue these concepts having no clue what they were and having no clue about what I was doing, but I would do it with all my might. I was like a shadow boxer and I won every round. I didn't get anywhere, but I won every round. I got a sense of *oh yeah!* That religious spirit came on and it felt good, but there was no lasting fruit! Finally, one day after another round of shadow boxing and realizing that I was getting nowhere, I said, "God this isn't making sense. I want everything You say is mine, but I'm frustrated. I don't know how to get there."

He said, "Well, quit."

"But God..."

"No Bruce, stop striving. I will do the work. You make the choice and I will make the change!"

You know what really was the cause of my frustration? What I thought I wanted was not happening in the manner I wanted it, nor was it happening as fast as I thought I should attain those desires. I was a product of my society, wanting everything now! But God's plan is perfect. His ways are not our ways, nor are His thoughts our thoughts. So I did what He told me: I quit!

"You shall keep the Sabbath, therefore, it is holy to you..." (Exod. 31:14a). It is holy to God and He says that it is to be regarded as holy to us.

> *Everyone who profanes it shall surely be put to death; for whoever does any work on it, that person shall be cut off from among his people* (Exodus 31:14-15).

For years I have been reiterating this fact: the arm of flesh will never accomplish the will of God. If we profane this Sabbath, this Seventh Day, spiritual death or separation from God will be the result. Yesterday's paradigm will not be effective in accomplishing the will of God on this day. The arm of flesh, humankind's attempts in their own strength and with their own understanding, will result in a spiritual Ishmael being birthed, rather than the will of God.

Rest in His Faith

We *must* enter into His rest on this day. The children of Israel wandered for 40 years in the wilderness; and because of unbelief, they did not enter into rest (see Heb. 4). It was not because they were not covenant people, and it was not because the Lord was not moving in their midst with unheard of miracles. It was because of their unbelief!

So many people say, "Well, if God did those miracles today, we would believe." Some would believe....that is true, but the majority of Christians cling to their unbelief as a well-known and well worn security blanket. After His resurrection, Jesus met upward of 500 people at one time (see 1 Cor. 15:6), and they witnessed the resurrected Christ personally. Now think of this: He told every one of those who had witnessed His resurrection to tarry in Jerusalem and await the promise of the Holy Ghost, but only 120 obeyed Him. We should not be so quick to speak about what we *would* do under certain circumstances, rather tell what we *are* doing!

Therefore the children of Israel shall keep the Sabbath, to observe the Sabbath throughout their generations as a perpetual covenant. It is a sign between Me and the children of Israel forever (Exodus 31:16-17).

Power of the Covenant

There are two major types of covenants found in the context of Scripture, and they can be summed up as such: a one-way covenant, which is unconditional; and a two-way covenant, which is conditional, based on the response of the individuals involved. Without writing a dissertation, we can explain covenants simply in this way: If I entered into a one-way covenant with an individual, I would say "Brother, I am going to do all this for you because I like you, and you do not have to do a thing in return." There would then be a covenantal agreement enacted through a ceremony of breaking of a shared meal. I would then be obligated to fulfill that covenant to the full extent of the commitment I made.

The second type of covenant enacted would be a two-way covenant. We enter into a covenant and exchange a meal, belts, and swords (I am simplifying as this is not my main focus), and there would be a shedding of blood. We, in essence, commit to exchange our strength for our covenant partner's strength, our inability for his ability, our lack for his abundance, and our life for his life. Now our enemies become his enemies and our battles his battles, and likewise, we take up his cause and remain faithful throughout our life and even into the lives of our offspring.

This is the type of covenant that the Lord established throughout all the generations as a perpetual covenant. The Lord is committed to fulfilling His covenant promises on the Seventh Day and the only thing He asks us to do is remember it and understand its purpose. We are going to enter into His rest. That is the covenant He has given us! How are we going to do that? Give up—cease from your own works and rely totally upon Him.

> *Then Moses gathered all the congregation of the children of Israel together, and said to them, "These are the words which the Lord has commanded you to do: work shall be done for six days, but the seventh day shall be a holy day for you, a Sabbath of rest to the Lord. Whoever does any work on it shall be put to death..." (Exodus 35:1-2).*

Deadly Fire of the Tongue

Again, spiritual death is the result of relying on the arm of flesh and adhering to the old model of ministry on the Seventh Day. Church as usual is not going to work.

Verse 3 says - *You shall kindle no fire throughout your dwellings on the Sabbath Day* (Exodus 35:3).

James 3:5-6 says, *Even so the tongue is a little member and boasts great things. See how great a forest a little fire kindles.*

The tongue is a fire, a world of iniquity. The tongue defiles the whole body and sets on fire the course of nature, and according to the Book of James, it is set on fire by hell!

On the Sabbath Day, *"You shall kindle no fire throughout your dwellings..."* (Exod. 35:3). If it takes the Lord having to come and sew our mouths shut, Lord, let it be done! You see, when He said *"among our members"* (James 3:6), He is talking about the Body of Christ, and we are the Body of Christ. We destroy each other with the words of our mouth. We kindle a fire in the bosom, in the heart, in the lives of everybody we come in contact with, when we speak death and not life and cursing and not blessing. But God is saying, *"In this day you shall kindle no fire in your dwelling, in your house"* (see

Exod. 35:3). We have to be a people of the Word of God who only speak when God says speak. We must stop criticizing, gossiping, slandering, condemning, and judging. It must stop, or we will never enter into the fullness of the promise of God.

The more we learn, the less we will speak. The more revelation He gives us, the more wisdom we will need before we open our mouths. Because this generation is being called and released during this season to walk under a greater weight of glory than past generations, we must understand this basic yet elusive truth; we must be slow to speak, slow to anger, and quick to listen (see James 1:19). Why? Because life and death are in the power of the tongue! (see Prov. 18:21). A creative force is released as you, the anointed of God, speak; whether it is a force for life or death.

Let me give you just one example. Do you know what the word *silly* means? Christians speak this over their children all the time. My wife Reshma caught me on this. *Silly* means "to be empty-headed and unwise." What did we just do when we called our child silly? We literally spoke, "you are an empty-headed unwise person." Our words carry real power, whether positive or negative; to release life and blessing or death and cursing.

Growing in God

Now extrapolate that example with the added understanding of the release of the promise of the Seventh Day. What happens as we grow in greater grace and anointing in this generation? The weight of our words will carry more power and will affect an even swifter change than before.

> *When I was a child, I spoke as a child, I understood as a child, I thought as a child; but when I became a man, I put away childish things* (1 Corinthians 13:11).

98

It is time to put away our childish ways and to grow up into Him in all things. It is a day of rest, covenant promise fulfilled and completion. We have a great opportunity before us of entering into the fullness of His promises—the decision is up to us.

We have to be a people of God's Word. We have to be a people who will yield and surrender our tongues to God. That does not mean we are perfect, but we must be quick to repent, slow to speak and slow to wrath.

If we repent of the things we speak that are not of God and do not bring life, we, in effect, stop their creative ability and they cease to exist. Put those past confessions and statements of unbelief under the blood. We must not "kindle fires" in our dwellings, in this temple, or the Body of Christ corporately, or in this world, on this Seventh Day!

Here is another example of how believers don't line up with what God says about them. The Word states, "*I can do all things through Christ who strengthens me*" (Phil. 4:13). That works for us, but usually with a clause or addendum attached: "well, I have got this sickness and I have got that ache; I don't have the money; I've never been to Bible college; I don't know how; I've got to be practical; the dog ate my homework...."

Let me give you a little rhyme the Lord gave me some years ago:

Only speak when spoken through
Only do what He tells you to do
Only go where He tells you to go
He'll let you know what you need to know.

We had a lady come to us during ministry in Malaysia some time ago. She was in a desperate state. She came and went on for ten minutes about all the negative things that were going on in her life. When she finally stopped and said, "Can you tell me why?" the

Lord began to give me some insight. So I shared with her what the Lord had shown me, and we prayed for her. When I was done, she said, "Well, you don't understand..." and once again she began to regal me with all the negative circumstances in her life. After the fourth time of going through this same cycle with her, in order to shock her and get her to listen, I finally said, "Okay, I agree with *you*. Forget what God said and go live in your misery." And I walked away.

I simply told her, "Look, I can agree with you, or you can agree with the Word. What do you want?" She finally got the message and, in effect, was willing to agree with the Word of God for her situation.

You see, we have to stop looking at our circumstances as the ultimate truth. They may be the facts of what we are facing at a given time, but the *truth* is what God says about us! What does the Word say about you? That is what you must speak! It does not matter what the world, your flesh, your mind, or your emotions say about you. What does the Word say about you? That is what you speak, that is what you believe, and that is what you must hold onto. You will never go wrong holding on to God's Word.

> *Six days shall work be done, but the seventh day is a Sabbath of solemn rest.... You shall do no work on it; it is the Sabbath of the Lord in all your dwellings* (Leviticus 23:3).

There will be a holy assembly on this Seventh Day. Not only do we need to recognize that our assembling together as the corporate Body of Christ wherever we meet is a holy convocation on this day, but we must look beyond our earthly gatherings and realize we are going home to be with the Lord on this day!

We have a friend, a brother in Christ, named Dean Braxton who in May of 2006 was declared to be clinically dead for an hour and 45 minutes. When he came back he made some interesting comments. At first, he couldn't find the words to express his experience. And when he was able to, the Lord told him not to say anything unless someone asked him a particular question regarding what he had seen. If he was asked, then he was permitted to tell them. So I began to ask him some questions based upon what I had experienced in my visitation to Heaven.

"Did you see such and such in Heaven?" I said.

"Yes."

"Well what about this?"

"Yes."

Once he realized my curiosity was based on similar experiences, he felt he had the freedom to share his own experience with me.

"You know what I found out up there? You can go there any time! Anyone who is a believer can go there any time!" Dean said.

I said, "Yes I know; it is in the Word." I showed him what the Word had to say about the access we as believers have to that realm.

He said, "There it is! I knew it was real because I have been there, but thank you!"

The most provocative statement he made to me was that Jesus is coming back sooner than we think. I cannot tell you how many times in our travels we've heard this same testimony from many people who have had these near-death experiences (I don't know why they are called "near death," since they died) or who have had a vision or visitation from the Lord. The testimony repeats and resounds; this is the generation that will witness the culmination of all that the Word has spoken—we will witness the return of Christ!

An Offering of Fire

Leviticus 23:7 says, *"You shall offer an offering made by fire to the Lord for seven days."* Now wait a minute, first we are not supposed to kindle any fire near our dwellings, but now we are supposed to give Him an offering made by fire?

Proverbs 27:21 says, *"The refining pot is for silver, and the furnace is for gold. Our God is a consuming fire."* The Lord is looking for an offering made by fire. God wants you tried seven times in that fire so you come forth pure and holy and righteous before Him. The Lord wants the offering of my life to be a willing sacrifice for Him. My response must be, "Lord, whatever it takes in my life to make me more like you, let it be so." If that means the fire of testing and trial must come and consumes every last ounce of my carnal nature, my flesh, so be it. This is the offering God wants in our lives right now. This is what the Lord is looking for. Let's give Him that offering on this Seventh Day.

Numbers 7:48 says, *On the seventh day Elishama (which means "the God who hears") the son of Ammihud...presented an offering.*

Verse 49 describes the offering as consisting of silver, money, flour, and oil. I want to focus on the offering of silver which equates to sanctification and redemption. What is the offering that you and I, as the people of God, can offer the Lord today? Does God need my money? As a child of God who has been redeemed by the blood of the Lamb, it is already all His. I am called to be a steward of finances. Does God need my car? The same argument applies: no; it is already His. The one thing the Lord *is* looking for is that we offer our hearts and our lives—all that is within us. That speaks of an offering of silver: sanctification.

"Lord, I offer myself to You to fulfill and complete the sanctification process in my life so I can become everything You have called me to be."

Let me encourage you, the Lord is doing a quick work on this Seventh Day. An acceleration is taking place. A process that once took years is not going to take years anymore. What will happen is, He will do a hundred years of work in a moment.

While traveling in Singapore and Malaysia, my wife and I have met some wonderful brothers and sisters in the Lord. Some of the more notable acquaintances have been a number of eight-year-olds who have been having supernatural encounters with the Lord and in some instances have been literally caught away in the spirit to Heaven to witness and communicate the heart of God for their generation. What is astounding is that in some instances a number of these children are coming back with an astonishing grasp and understanding of Scripture, and they are teaching and preaching with profound wisdom.

Washing of the Water

I've said this before and I'll say it once again: One moment in the presence of the King is worth a thousand years of earthly study! No comparison can adequately convey this simple yet profound truth.

Numbers 19:11-12 says, *He who touches the dead body of anyone shall be unclean for seven days. He shall purify himself with water on the third day and on the seventh day; then he will be clean.*

Water is a type of the Word of God. It is the washing of the water of the Word. Water also is a type of the Spirit. I cannot say this enough: Don't touch the unclean thing—do not be a partaker of another person's sins. Guard your hearts and guard your testimony by being aware of those whom you labor among. Let there be no appearance of evil.

Do not lay hands suddenly on anybody. Listen to what the Spirit is telling you, and realize that what we did yesterday is not necessarily what we are supposed to do today. Don't get stuck in a formula or a pattern on how you pray for people. Be led of the Spirit!

We have to purify ourselves with the washing of the water on the third day and the Seventh Day. These two days are in conjunction. It is the third day removed from Jesus, and the Seventh Day removed from Adam. The prophetic fulfillment of each of these Seventh-Day Scriptures is unfolding in our generation, and our response will have an impact upon our future.

> Numbers 19:19 says, *The clean person shall sprinkle the unclean on the third day and on the seventh day; and on the seventh day he shall purify himself, wash his clothes, and bathe in water, and at evening he will be clean.*

Evangelists take note: this is the day of the great harvest! Multitudes who are in the valley of decision will be harvested on this day as we obey the great commission! On the Seventh Day, it is time for us to immerse ourselves in the Word of God and in the God of the Word. We can then release that washing of the water of the Word to other people.

An interesting aspect of this washing of the water of the Word in my life is that in the last couple of years there have been a number of people who, when they have come up for prayer for healing, I instantly know the symptoms are symptomatic of sin in their life. That had never happened before. What I have been led to do is this: I go to James 5, where the Lord said if I pray the prayer of faith it saves the sick and their sins are forgiven (see James 5:15). I pray something like this, "Father, their sins are forgiven in the name of Jesus," and I apply the blood of Jesus. Where, in the past, healing was difficult to effect, I have been seeing a greater release of healing than ever before in the lives of needy individuals.

Healing the Harvest

My question then becomes one of retaining the healing. How do we keep them healed? The washing of the water of the Word—teach, instruct, and trust. Teach them God's Word; instruct them in righteousness; and trust God to do it.

Mark 2:23 says, "*Now it happened that Jesus went through the grainfields on the Sabbath….*" What are the grain fields? The grain fields are the fields the Lord said were already ripe unto harvest. Do not say there are yet four months to the harvest. I tell you that right now the fields are ripe (see John 4:35). They are ready for harvesting. All over the world, we anticipate a harvest coming, and its full release is contingent upon our obedient response to the great commission.

Continuing with verse 23; …*as they went His disciples began to pluck the heads of grain.*

A hunger resonates within the heart of the Lord as He anticipates the final harvest of the earth; a longing for the fulfillment of the promised inheritance that belongs to Jesus, namely, the nations of the world. And those who are walking intimately with the Lord understand the times and the seasons and hunger for this complete redemption to take place.

I used to think evangelism was standing on the street corner handing out tracts, and I've got to be honest, that never worked for me because I was shy. There was no way I was doing that. I was in bondage to the fear of humanity. When I realized that ministry is more about relationship with the Lord and doing what *He* tells you to do, rather than feeling obligated to the programs that have been instituted by humankind, I was able to flow in the gifting the Lord had given me. In doing so, I became more effective in my witness for Christ.

Right now a harvest is taking place. Millions of people all over the earth are having a face-to-face encounter with Jesus, and He's saying, *"I am the way the truth and the life, follow me"* (see John 14:16). Why would He do that? It's the Seventh Day, and Jesus and His disciples are walking through the fields that are ripe unto harvest—and they are plucking those heads of grain because they are hungry!

Ali's Divine Encounter

An Iranian man named Ali immigrated in the late 1990s to the United States and lived in California. Ali was busy working when one night Jesus appeared to him and he was radically saved and filled with the Holy Ghost. He had absolutely no paradigm for that type of experience in his belief system (nor do most Christians). So he purchased a Bible and started reading. He didn't know much about attending church, so he continued with worshiping God and praying in the Spirit.

A couple of years after he received Jesus into his heart, he had a supernatural dream, and in that dream he saw himself not living in California any longer but living back in the Midwest working for his uncle in his store. His dream continued and he remembers sharing with his uncle the truth of Jesus being the one true God, about the tribulation, and all these things that were coming upon the nations during the end of the age, but his uncle would have nothing to do with it.

The next thing that happened in his dream is he saw himself suddenly caught up in the air to be with Jesus. While this was happening, his heart broke because his uncle was standing and weeping because now he realized everything that Ali told him was true, and he now had to go through the tribulation. Ali then woke up from the dream and thought, "What was that?" So he went to the Bible and started studying. Ali understands from that experience that the catching of the Body of Christ is imminent and is sooner than we know.

Two years after his dream, Ali got a call from his uncle who said, "Ali, can you come back and work for me? I need your help to run my store!" So soon Ali was back in the Midwest, in the city he had seen in his dream, working in his uncle's store where he saw himself being caught up in what the Church calls the rapture.[1]

The harvest is ripe right now—and Jesus Himself is walking in the harvest fields and He is harvesting. In some of the nations we have traveled, we have met Muslims to whom Jesus has appeared and they were saved. The latest one we met at a home meeting. The couple that had the house said that their Muslim maid from Indonesia told them this story: She was by herself while her employers were away, when all of a sudden, out of nowhere, a man came down the stairs all dressed in white.

The maid said, "Who are you?"

He answered, "Ask your employer."

So when they came home, she said, "This man appeared on the staircase and he was dressed all in white, who was He?" and she went on to describe him.

They were able to tell her the truth of the Gospel and about Jesus, and she was saved.

In another incident on Christmas day, a Christian family was at their church service. The maid, who was unsaved and a Muslim, was at home and she saw a man in white walking down the hall.

She said, "Who are you?"

He said, "My name is Jesus. I am the Way, the Truth, and the Life, follow me."

So on Christmas day she was given the greatest gift of all—eternal life!

This is happening all over the earth. Why? It is because the harvest is ripe and it is the Seventh Day! The Pharisees, the traditionalists, say "Look what they are doing! It is not lawful to do that on the Sabbath. God doesn't do that anymore! We know that is not the biblical Jesus appearing to people."

Yet Jesus responds now as He did then, "*Have you never read what David did when he was in need and hungry?*" (Mark 2:25). Being in need and hungry indicates a person who is passionate. It is not that I am privileged to preach the Gospel, which I am; it is not that I want to, no, I am compelled! The Word of God is like fire shut up in my bones, and I am compelled. I have a need, to see men and women of God released into their destiny in this hour. I am passionate and I am hungry to see the fulfillment of this because I want Jesus to come back. It is not just, "Well, yeah that sounds fun." It used to be that way with me. Now it is a burning desire.

And He said to them, "The Sabbath was made for man, and not man for the Sabbath. Therefore the Son of Man is also Lord of the Sabbath" (Mark 2:27-28).

This Sabbath was made for us. Specifically for this generation, even more specifically, it is for you! The Son of Man is the Lord of The Seventh Day. We are about to see a release of the Lordship of Jesus Christ in the earth, in our lives, and in our gatherings unlike anything we have ever witnessed or experienced before. We are going to experience a measure of His rule in our lives that will transcend every other experience or understanding that we have embraced in the past. This is the Seventh Day, and He will be glorified!

ENDNOTE

1. Christine Darg, *Miracles Among Muslims* (Pescara, IT: Destiny Image Europe Publishers, 2007).

CHAPTER 6

Fresh Faith

I am constantly being overwhelmed and amazed by what the Lord is revealing on a daily basis from His Word for this generation. As we look at the story of the crossing over into the Promised Land found in Joshua chapter six, we have a perfect example. The Lord spoke to Joshua as the leader of the children of Israel and told him that they were to cross the Jordan on the third day (see Josh. 3:2). The meaning of the name Jordan is "death and descending." It can also be viewed as the final obstacle on the journey of the children of Israel before entering into the fullness of the promise of God spoken prophetically over them for generations. As we look into this passage of Scripture, we will find parallels to our day and some of the hindrances keeping us from our Promised Land on this Seventh Day.

Death to Old Thinking

Of necessity, there will need to be a "death" to some of our previous mind-sets on how to see the purposes of God accomplished in our lives. We will have to divorce ourselves from any practice that has become habitual in following the Lord and learn to rely totally upon the leading of His Spirit. This will take a measure of humility (descending) in recognizing that some of our previous methods of doing things were, at best, humanity's attempt to bring to pass the promises of God, and at worst, blatant attempts to thwart the reality of those promises in our lives. To put it simply, the Jordan River literally speaks of that which keeps you, or hinders you, or blocks you from entering into your promise on this Seventh Day.

> *And the Lord said to Joshua: "See! I have given Jericho into your hand, its king, and the mighty men of valor. You shall march around the city, all you men of war; you shall go all around the city once. This you shall do six days. And seven priests shall bear seven trumpets of rams' horns before the ark. But the seventh day you shall march around the city seven times, and the priests shall blow the trumpets. It shall come to pass, when they make a long blast with the ram's horn, and when you hear the sound of the trumpet, that all the people shall shout with a great shout; then the wall of the city will fall down flat. And the people shall go up every man straight before him." Then Joshua the son of Nun called the priests and said to them, "Take up the ark of the covenant, and let seven priests bear seven trumpets of rams' horns before the ark of the Lord." And he said to the people, "Proceed, and march around the city, and let him who is armed advance before the ark of the Lord." So it was, when Joshua had spoken to the people, that the seven priests bearing the seven trumpets of rams' horns before the Lord advanced and blew the trumpets, and the ark of the covenant of the Lord followed them. The armed men went before the priests who blew the trumpets, and the rear guard came after the ark, while the priests continued blowing the trumpets. Now Joshua had commanded the people, saying, "You shall not shout or make any noise with your voice, nor shall a word proceed out of your mouth, until the*

day I say to you, 'Shout!' Then you shall shout." So he had the ark of the Lord circle the city, going around it once. Then they came into the camp and lodged in the camp. And Joshua rose early in the morning, and the priests took up the ark of the Lord. Then seven priests bearing seven trumpets of rams' horns before the ark of the Lord went on continually and blew with the trumpets. And the armed men went before them. But the rear guard came after the ark of the Lord, while the priests continued blowing the trumpets. And the second day they marched around the city once and returned to the camp. So they did six days.

But it came to pass on the seventh day that they rose early, about the dawning of the day, and marched around the city seven times in the same manner. On that day only they marched around the city seven times. And the seventh time it happened, when the priests blew the trumpets, that Joshua said to the people: "Shout, for the Lord has given you the city!" (Joshua 6:2-16).

You will notice in Joshua chapter 3, it was the act of obediently following the leading and presence of God that removed the obstacle (the waters of the Jordan) for the children of Israel so they could enter into the Promised Land. The Lord told Joshua to have the priests go before the children of Israel with the Ark of the Covenant (or the presence of God) on their shoulders. When their feet stepped into the water, the waters would be parted. There is revelation in this for our life that pertains to this moment in history. First, we must be able to hear the voice of God. If we are not able to hear His voice, it is impossible to obey His voice.

Second, when the Lord speaks we must be obedient. As those priests took a step of faith they did not know exactly what was going to happen. They just knew the Lord had given direction and they were to obey. They found this truth to be evident: God inhabits what He commands. Immediately when the presence of the Lord came into contact with that which withheld the promise of God from their lives, the obstacle was removed. And His presence was released through the faithful obedience displayed by the priests stepping into the water. We will also see the Lord make a way for us where there seems to be no way as we respond in obedience to what He is saying in this hour. I don't know what the promise is that God has given you for your life specifically, but the path is opened before you by obedience to His Word. Without that initial step of faith, you will never see the obstacles removed from your path.

Covenant of Circumcision

You will also note that this generation had to enter into a covenant of circumcision for this new move of God. The strategies and abilities of past generations were not going to carry this generation forward into the fulfillment of the promise. This circumcision indicates a circumcising of our hearts in preparation for moving into a new season of spiritual warfare and victory. It is a preparation that is necessary for continued transformation and sanctification, preparing us for our journey toward destiny. The generation that perished in the wilderness whom God brought out of Egypt with a strong right arm became examples of what *not* to do. Because of their murmuring and bickering, and speaking against the leadership that God had established, they wandered in that wilderness for 40 years and they never entered their promise. Unbelief was and is the cause of continually wandering in places of wilderness, and it will keep us out of our promised land if we do not allow the Holy Spirit to complete the process of sanctification in our lives.

When there is gossip or slander, when judgment is cast, when there is continual complaining, it is because of unbelief, and it will keep us from fulfilling our destiny.

We see the Lord presenting a new strategy for this new day. Let's examine Joshua 6:1, *"Now Jericho was securely shut up because of the children of Israel. None went out and none came in."* The first obstacle the children of Israel came to in their promised land was a fortified city named Jericho. This was a city that had never seen its walls breached, nor had it ever suffered defeat at the hands of an opposing army. It was a bastion that was shut up securely against any attempts to overcome and take or destroy it. It was an enemy stronghold that if not defeated would hinder the rest of Israel's campaign in taking their Promised Land. It had to be defeated, and yet, it seemed to the natural mind to be an insurmountable obstacle.

We find only one thing that will allow any of us to enter into our destiny: obedience to the voice of God. We have to be able to hear His voice, and when we hear it, we must be obedient to what He tells us to do, no matter how foolish it looks. To the natural mind, what God told these people to do was absolutely ludicrous. It was contrary to every known application of warfare in their day.

The Lord said to Joshua in Joshua 6:2 that He had already given this land and its kings and its people into Joshua's hand. He virtually told him it's a done deal; it's yours. *Your* destiny is already complete in Him. What God has promised you for your life is already done in His eyes. The victory is already accomplished. The question is how to get from where we're at—where victory looks impossible—to where God says I am to be? By obedience! Whatever God calls you to in life, whatever you are facing, the victory is yours. What you need is a strategy from Heaven, and the only way you can get that is to hear from the Lord.

The Lord told the Israelites, Here is your strategy. March around the city with all your men of war, one time each day for six days (see Joshua 6:3).

Again, six is the number of man. For 6,000 years—six days—with our own strength of arms and with our finite understanding, we have tried to accomplish or fulfill the promise of God for our lives. We have had some measure of success, but as a whole, we have fallen short of the high calling of God for our lives. How do I know that? Just look at the character of the Church. There has been a lot of rhetoric and yet the fruit of the spirit evidenced by character is nonexistent or shallow at best. If Christ-like character and if the fruit of the Spirit became foundational in the life of every believer, a supernatural transformation would take place in the world. I know we all have to grow into these facets of the character of Christ, however, for the most part, we have seen more lack of character in the Church than we have seen in the world. But thank God it is the Seventh Day and the Lord is changing us! The Scripture says Jesus is coming back for a Church that is without spot or blemish! We are in a season of character redevelopment and the development of the fruit of the spirit in our collective lives as we move forward into our Seventh-Day destiny.

In Joshua 6:7, the Lord told Joshua to have *"Seven priests bear seven trumpets…before the ark of the Lord."* *Seven* again, in biblical numerology, refers to "rest, covenant promise fulfilled, and completion." In essence, the Lord is saying that a company of priests who are in complete rest will move according to the mandate of Heaven and will make prophetic proclamation in His presence (the ark), and they will see this promise come to pass on the Seventh Day! We are a royal priesthood before Him, and we are going to see the *Jerichos* in our lives destroyed on this Seventh Day in obedience to the leading of the Spirit of God.

Again, the Lord said, "Seven priests shall bear seven trumpets of rams' horns before the Ark." Allegorically, trumpets speak of a prophetic voice. So we have priests and prophets sounding the alarm and speaking forth, and they are going before the presence of God, the Ark. These signs will follow those who believe... Because they believed God and they took a step of faith, the Lord did what He said he was going to do. These signs *will* follow those who believe:

> *And seven priests shall bear seven trumpets of rams' horns before the Ark. But the seventh day, you shall march around the city seven times, and the priests shall blow the trumpets. It shall come to pass when they make a long blast with the ram's horns, and when you hear the sound of the trumpet, that all the people shall shout with a great shout; then the wall of the city will fall down flat. And the people shall go up every man straight before him.*" (Joshua 6:4-5)

That is not how you win a war! That is not how you lay siege to a city. You use swords and arrows and oil and fire. You build siege engines and you cut off supplies and water to the city. Everything the Lord spoke to them, His new strategy, was contrary to the natural order of things and was outside the realm of the reasonable as far as the natural man was concerned. In my own experience, I have been not a little bit amused, as well as concerned, at the attempts of believers to develop formulas for prayer and spiritual warfare. We have seen well-meaning people in their efforts to find a simple solution to spiritual warfare come up with some of the most bizarre concepts. They can give you 37 steps on how to effectively change the atmosphere of a city, see people delivered, restore homes and family, etc. While on the surface, some of these plans may have been commissioned and given by the Lord, we take them and peddle them wholesale to the Body of Christ as if we now have *the* solution. What we have done is take a strategy that was effective in one battle and packaged it for use in every battle. That is not how to be led of the Spirit! Even in the natural world, each battle in a war is dynamic and needs up-to-the-moment insight and strategy development to gain victory.

Beware of Principles of Witchcraft

In spiritual matters we have found that patterns and formulas equal witchcraft. The principles of God's Word are sound. Principles are a foundation and a basis on which we are to be established and move forward. But the principles of the Word are always subject to the voice of God and *how-to* implementation of God. When we take principles and make them patterns and formulas, we step out of the realm of possibility and into the realm of flesh. We remove God from the equation. But if we stay in the realm of the spirit, principles will remain just that—principles. We then obey the voice of the Lord and hear how to apply those principles to each circumstance or situation, and we see something supernatural happen. The major principle to remember in every spiritual battle is simply to obey and follow the leading of the Spirit.

> *Then Joshua the son of Nun called the priests and said to them, "Take up the ark of the covenant, and let seven priests bear seven trumpets of rams' horns before the Ark of the Lord."* (Joshua 6:6)

The narrative indicates that Joshua did not argue with the Lord or this unusual strategy. His was an astounding response, unless you realize the extent of Joshua's relationship with the Lord. Throughout Moses' life, Joshua served the leader of his people with a singleness of purpose and passion and a great desire to know God. Oftentimes, when Moses would leave the tent of meeting or when he came down from Mt. Sinai, Joshua would remain in the presence of the Lord. His passion, hunger, and trust in God came through an intimate relationship developed as he served the man of God named Moses. Because of this relationship and his ability to recognize the voice of God, Joshua did not waver in his obedience to what he heard.

The Walls of Jericho

Let me share with you some historical and archeological facts about Jericho. The walls of Jericho could have eight chariots riding abreast across the wall. These walls were approximately 40 feet high and had never been breached. Foreign kings and their armies had come against the city but they all left in defeat because of the impenetrability of this fortress city.

According to the biblical narrative, the walls of Jericho were pushed down, literally into the ground. When archeologists finally excavated ancient Jericho, they found to their amazement that the biblical account of the walls being pushed into the ground to be correct! Most of the blocks used in the walls were huge and they found in the center of each block a compartment full of children's bones. It was belief of the Jericho people that if they offered their children to the false god Molech and placed their bones inside each block, they would never be breached or defeated. And they weren't…until they met God. This was considered to be an impregnable fortress. Nobody had ever defeated Jericho until a bunch of wandering tribesmen with a covenant-keeping God came out of the desert and across the flooded Jordan River.

Perfect Faith

Unbelief in your life will keep you in the wilderness of despair and will eventually lead you to an unfulfilled grave. Unbelief modeled by the previous generation in Joshua's time saw those initially called to take the Promised Land die in the wilderness, never having obtained their promise. Faith is not the absence of doubt but the presence of belief in the midst of doubt. The fruit of a lifestyle of doubt is evident in habitual complaining, slandering, bickering, and gossiping. Remember the man in the New Testament, who said, *"Lord, I believe; help my unbelief"* (Mark 9:24)? Faith is *not* the absence of doubt, but actively using what faith you have in the midst of doubt. If faith were the absence of doubt, there would not be a human being alive today and there would never be a "fight of faith" necessary in obtaining any promise.

Nobody has perfect faith without some doubt that encroaches and tries to come against him or her. I used to struggle with faith, because I was taught that you have to build up your faith and once you get to a certain level of "bionic" (or so it seemed) faith, you can do anything! So I was always fighting to keep away any minuscule sense of doubt in my life. We grow in faith, but we do so by using the measure of faith we have. To think otherwise leads to a sense of inadequacy and ultimately failure.

The Lord said in Matthew 17:20 ...*for verily I say unto you, If ye have faith as a grain of mustard seed, ye shall say unto this mountain, Remove hence to yonder place; and it shall remove; and nothing shall be impossible unto you* (KJV).

He did not say you needed mountain-size faith to move a mountain. No; you just need a little bit. It doesn't matter what you face in your life, whatever amount of faith you've got, it is enough for you to win through to victory. You have enough to do anything God says to do.

Jesus said in John 14:12, *Verily, verily, I say unto you, He that believeth on me, the works that I do shall he do also; and greater works than these shall he do; because I go unto my Father* (KJV).

John 1:3 says, *All things were made by him; and without him was not anything made that was made* (KJV).

Supernatural Authority

Now, if we are to believe that John 14:12 is the Word of God and truth, then we must understand we have a creative ability within us according to John 1:3 that has never been grasped nor understood. We have an untapped creative potential within us that literally shapes our world; namely our words. God invested in you, His power— dynamic, life-changing, world-changing power. You just have to believe it.

Let me give you another example of the authority of the believer. There was a pastor in Oklahoma living in what they call Tornado Alley. It was tornado season, so he had his radio on while he was working in his office, and he heard the emergency broadcast signal indicating there was a funnel cloud forming. When they gave the location of this impending tornado he said, "Wait a minute, that's right above my church!" He ran outside and he looked up and there was this funnel cloud coming down. As he looked at it he said, "No way! You go up in the name of Jesus." And it went up!

Then it started coming down again and he said, "No, go up, in the name of Jesus!" And it went up again! The third time it started coming down he got a little angry. He yelled, "I told you, in the name of Jesus go back up and dissipate!" And it disappeared. Now how much faith did he have? He only had mustard-seed size faith, yet he could stop a tornado.

We do not realize what is resident within us. Sometimes it takes us getting pushed into the corner where we have no recourse but to come out swinging. That is unfortunate. The truth, however, is that what Jesus did, He said we can do also. I love that He said "The works that *I do*," not "the works that I did" (see John 14:12). The "works" He *is* doing right now, you can do and even greater works than these. Get this in your spirit: Jesus did not say the works that he did 2,000 years ago you can do, although that is part of the whole; He said the works that I do! He is speaking to us in the present tense of His existence. That takes us to a whole new level and realm of possibility!

Heaven on Earth

Now what we have to do is discover what God is doing *today.* As I listen to the testimonies from all over the world today and hear of the interaction of Heaven into the lives of people, I am encouraged to believe the Lord for greater things. As we shared earlier, He is visiting people all over the world and calling them unto Himself. He is raising the dead. He is releasing men and women from spiritual, emotional, and physical bondage. He is reconciling families—husbands and wives, children and parents—to one another. The list goes on and on. What He *is* doing, we can do! I am challenged by His Word continually to believe for other than what I've seen modeled in the Church at large.

> For instance, Matthew 10:7-8 says, *And as you go, preach, saying, "The kingdom of heaven is at hand." Heal the sick, cleanse the lepers, raise the dead, cast out demons. Freely you have received, freely give.*

Notice the Word did not say you cannot heal the sick; you cannot cleanse the lepers, you cannot raise the dead, or you cannot cast out demons. No, He said to do so freely. It is interesting to note that Jesus did not say heal only certain types of sickness. He did not say cleanse only a particular type of leprosy, nor did He say you are only to raise those who have been dead that were Christians or have been interred for a certain amount of time only. He did not indicate only certain types of demonic possession or oppression were the limit of His authority in us.

He put no limitation on any of this. As I read and understand it, we can raise the dead no matter if they were saved or unsaved;

no matter if they have been deceased a day, a week, a month, or a year. Jesus did not put a limitation upon this—we do! Before we go off half cocked, let me add this: We are to be led of the Spirit of God and do as He instructs us.

> Joshua 6:7-8 says, *And He said to the people, "Proceed, and march around the city, and let him who is armed advance before the Ark of the Lord." So it was, when Joshua had spoken to the people, that the seven priests bearing the seven trumpets of rams' horns before the Lord advanced and blew the trumpets, and the ark of the covenant of the Lord followed them.*

There was a sound, a prophetic voice, released into the atmosphere. Notice that He said let the armed men precede the Ark also. So we have the priests with the trumpets and the armed men going before the Ark of the Covenant. Those who were not armed followed the Ark. Are you spiritually prepared for the generation in which you live? Have you been armed by God's Word, by the Spirit of God, and led by the presence of God? As we become a people who immerse ourselves in the presence of God and in the God of the Presence; as we become a people who yearn for and desire the deeper things of God, we become armed, prepared, and ready. Then signs will follow us, wherever we are led.

The Sound of Victory

> Joshua 6:9-10 says, *The armed men went before the priests and who blew the trumpets, and the rear guard came after the ark, while the priests continued blowing the trumpets. Now Joshua had commanded the people, saying, "you shall not shout or make any noise with your voice, nor shall a word proceed out of your mouth until the day I say to you, "Shout!" Then you shall shout."*

This would absolutely take a miracle today. Even when I was in the military and we had to stand in formation and nobody was supposed to move or speak, even in that atmosphere you get those who cannot listen, be obedient, or do what they are told. And that was after intense indoctrination and training.

The strategy for Joshua's Seventh-Day victory was obedience and silence! For 40 years in the wilderness, the people had murmured, complained, and gossiped. For 40 years they had sown the seeds of discord and defeat with their mouths. In essence, the Lord was saying, "I am giving you a new strategy for this new day. You were unable to grasp the authority of your own tongue in the past, so in this day you will keep your mouth shut! You will speak only upon My command and you will say only what I tell you to say!"

On only one occasion have I ever seen a *holy hush* descend upon a congregation, and it lasted an hour and ten minutes! I believe, to date, that was one of the most profound miracles I have witnessed! It was an act of God. Yet, we are given the privilege of learning to keep still before Him! How will we ever learn what it means to "Be still and know that I am God!" (Ps. 46:10)

We have lost the art of listening prayer. There was a time when many congregations would gather and wait upon the Lord in silence. This was practiced in the late 1800s and early 1900s. Believers would come and wait on God and listen. They wouldn't do anything until the Lord spoke, and when He spoke, they would be obedient to what He said in that moment. We need to get back to the place of not being nervous in the place of silent waiting! We need to cultivate an atmosphere of rest on this Seventh Day where *being* is more important than *doing*. From this place of rest we will go forth led of the Spirit of God armed with new strategies and releasing His Kingdom purposes upon the earth.

Let me tell you something about Jericho. One of the meanings of the word *Jericho* is "recompense of reward." How do we receive that recompense of reward? Through obedience—by doing what the Lord says. In preparing ourselves for this day, we arm ourselves for battle. That means immersing ourselves in the Word of God and the God of the Word, and then speaking when spoken through. It is in so doing that we will receive great reward.

On the Seventh Day, spiritual warfare will be radically different than anything we have ever experienced before. This is the hour when our God is going to fight for us! All we have to do is be obedient and only speak what He tells us to speak. Remember, it was because of disobedience that the Israelites spent 40 years in the wilderness of murmuring, bickering, complaining, and backbiting. Forty years of nothing but negativity and death proceeded out of their mouths, and they reaped what they had sown. We are realizing a new strategy for this new day. The Lord is saying to keep our mouths shut, unless He releases us to speak! That is love, not judgment. It was the love of the Father that told them to be silent marching around Jericho because He knew what was in humankind.

A Lesson in Silence

Remember that no false fire will be kindled in your dwelling on the Seventh Day. What is the false fire? It is the tongue of iniquity. Look what a great fire a little ember can kindle. The tongue is a great fire. We have to learn how to keep our mouths shut and only speak when spoken through.

The Lord wants to teach us something new on this Seventh Day: a new mode of spiritual warfare—in addition to keeping our mouths shut, He wants us to be led by the Spirit. Speak when spoken through. Only do what He tells you to do!

We must go back to the place of knowing our Lord intimately so that we will know His voice. If we do not know His voice, then it is hard to do what He says. Jesus said, "I only do what I see my Father doing" (see John 5:19). If we can't see what the Father is doing, and we can't hear what He is saying, we are never going to enter into our destiny. Thank God that He is removing obstacles to our destiny! Our Jordan river, that hindrance that has kept us from the Promised Land, the Lord will supernaturally remove for those who submit to the process of sanctification and yield their members (their body—to include their tongue) to Him on this Seventh Day.

We *are* a terminal generation: terminal in the sense that we are moving from one realm of glory to another, from one measure of existence to a greater measure of existence. We *are* going to be complete! We will become the Church that is without spot or wrinkle before Jesus returns! (See Ephesians 5:26-28.) I'm so convinced of this in my heart that words fail me in an attempt to express this. Scores of people all over the world have been relaying to us that the Lord spoke to them that they are going to see the return of Jesus in their lifetime. All over the world, I have been hearing this, and I personally have known this in my heart since I was four years of age. As strange as that sounds, I remember when we lived in an apartment and my brother and sister and I were playing in the living room. Suddenly, experiencing an instant understanding of prophetic significance, I stopped playing. Having no knowledge nor understanding of whom I was talking about, I said, "It is going to be neat to be here when Jesus comes back!" They looked at me, and said, "Who is that?" I said, "I don't know!" But I knew of a certainty it was a fact. (I've had many prophetic experiences as a child that came to pass as I perceived and saw them to be.)

I *know* that I know that I'm going to see the return of the King. I'm hearing it all over the world, especially from young children.[1]

I met an eight-year-old in Singapore who had a supernatural experience. She was caught away in the spirit into the third heaven and had a glorious encounter with the Lord. Her testimony was, "He's coming, get ready it's sooner than you can even imagine!"

The Seventh Day is the dawning of a release of new strategies from Heaven in order to take the Promised Land the Lord declares is ours. It is a day we will see the fulfillment and completion of the promises for our lives fulfilled as we rely wholly upon Him in all that we do. It is a day of "no more posturing"; but a day of becoming all that He repeatedly says we are in His Word. It is a day of the realization of entering into His rest. It is a day of victory in the midst of impossibility and apprehension in the midst of an elusive goal—Christ-likeness.

ENDNOTE

1. Visit www.Sidroth.org, then go to his "It's Supernatural" show and look under the archives. You will find many interviews with people who have died, gone to Heaven, come back, and reported, "This is the generation!" That includes twelve-year-olds, all the way to those in their sixties.

CHAPTER 7

Prophetic Intercession

It came to pass on the seventh day that they rose early, about the dawning of the day... (Joshua 6:15).

I t was early in the morning on the Seventh Day that the camp of Israel arose to enter into their destiny. Right now, prophetically speaking, we are early in the morning on the Seventh Day. The Lord is releasing new strategies from Heaven for you and me to enter into the promise of God for our lives, and to conquer anything that stands in our path. It is a supernatural season of unusual miracles to which we have been called. We will not see the fulfillment of this destiny with a program designed according to the understanding of previous moves of God, nor by a doctrinal edict or resolution. We will not see a mixture of flesh and spirit attesting to man's involvement in this season. We will have the opportunity to be witness to the most all-encompassing and pervasive move of God ever experienced by the world.

Obedience in All Things

We will only participate to the extent we learn to be obedient to the Lord in all things. As we yield to His Spirit and walk this walk of obedience, we will see the walls of our Jericho destroyed;

and we will overcome every obstacle that hinders our progress. Whatever is keeping you from your destiny, early in the morning on this Seventh Day, God is going to release a strategy to you, and you will have the opportunity, through obedience, of entering into that destiny. I will guarantee you that the strategy you receive will in some way seem ludicrous or virtually impossible to sound reason. I have never had the Lord instruct me to do something for Him that required the absence of faith. Everything I have been asked of God to do was usually well beyond my own ability, which caused me to pursue Him and exercise my faith to see the fruition of what He called me to do. Again, He never asks us to do something that doesn't stretch us or that is not beyond our limited understanding. He always asks us to do something that requires faith in Him, because anything that is not of faith is sin.

Breaking Through to Destiny

Breakthrough is the operative word for your destiny today. This is a day in which every obstacle to the Body of Christ becoming the head and not the tail, above and not beneath, will be removed. The plans and purposes of God will culminate in our generation as we see the coming forth of a Bride that is without spot or blemish.

Joshua 6:15 says, *It came to pass on the seventh day that they rose early, about the dawning of the day, and marched around the city seven times in the same manner.*

On that day only, according to the command of the Lord, they marched around the city seven times. On the seventh time around they let out a resounding prophetic shout of victory that terrified the enemy and released the power of Heaven that pushed those walls into the ground. I believe that prophetic shout released the host of Heaven to facilitate the removal of the barrier (the walls of Jericho) to total victory. The strategy the Lord is releasing to you and me, when acted upon in obedience, will activate the host of Heaven on our behalf, and we will see absolute victory in the face of what looks like the inevitability of hopeless defeat.

> *And they utterly destroyed all that was in the city, both man and woman, young and old, ox and sheep and donkey, with the edge of the sword* (Joshua 6:21).

They destroyed everything that was considered unclean within that city with the edge of the sword. There was to be no compromise with the unfruitful works of darkness because a little leaven would contaminate the whole camp of Israel. As we are obedient to the Lord in our lives, we will see the strategies of the enemy destroyed with the edge of the sword—the Word of God that proceeds out of our mouth! It must be in obedience to what the Lord has commanded us that causes us to speak. Anything else will be a work of the flesh and will further hinder our destiny.

> *But they burned the city and all that was in it with fire. Only the silver and gold, and the vessels of bronze and iron, they put into the treasury of the house of the Lord* (Joshua 6:24).

Notice it says that the silver and gold, as well as the vessels of bronze and iron, were reaped as spoils and were put into the treasury of the house of the Lord. This is an example of how the economy of Heaven will operate at the end of the age. We must understand we have been called to be stewards of whatever the Lord puts into our hands. It all belongs to Him! There will be no self-enrichment or building of individual kingdoms in this hour. We will be participants in establishing the Kingdom of God on the earth. The Lord will provide our needs according to His riches in glory, not according to the manipulative and coercive tactics of professional hucksters trying to build their own kingdoms.

We have to come to the revelation of this hour! The favor of God, the blessing of God, the Word of God, the armies of God, and this fullness of time season all are on our side! We cannot lose, unless we choose to do so! We have had a *we-can't-win* mentality in the past because the obstacles in our path seemed insurmountable. But I want you to know: The bigger the hindrance, the harder it will fall! This is the Seventh Day—a day of breakthrough and release!

I love the story of David and Goliath. The Israeli army all said, "That giant is so big. How can we win?" But David said, "He's so big, how can I miss?" We must view our challenges in this hour with the same spirit of might that David displayed. The target is so big, how can we miss? If God is for us, who can be against us?

Taking Down Samson

Now let's look at another example of the promise of the Seventh Day:

And it happened, when they saw him, that they brought thirty companions to be with him. Then Samson said to them, "Let me pose a riddle to you. If you can correctly solve and explain it to me within the seven days of the feast, then I will give you thirty linen garments and thirty changes of clothing. But if you cannot explain it to me, then you shall give me thirty linen garments and thirty changes of clothing." And they said to him, "Pose your riddle, that we may hear it." So he said to them: "Out of the eater came something to eat, And out of the strong came something sweet." Now for three days they could not explain the riddle. But it came to pass on the seventh day that they said to Samson's wife, "Entice your husband, that he may explain the riddle to us, or else we will burn you and your father's house with fire. Have you invited us in order to take what is ours? Is that not so?" Then Samson's wife wept on him, and said, "You only hate me! You do not love me! You have posed a riddle to the sons of my people, but you have not explained it to me." And he said to her, "Look, I have not explained it to my father or my mother; so should I explain it to you?" Now she had wept on him the seven days while their feast lasted. And it happened on the seventh day that he told her, because she pressed him so much. Then she explained the riddle to the sons of her people (Judges 14:11-17).

This is the story of Samson, a man of destiny who was called and consecrated from his mother's womb to the purposes of God. However, in the spirit of compromise and contrary to the law of God not to take a wife of any foreign culture, Samson became engaged to a Philistine woman. It seems that Samson also habitually ignored his vows as a Nazarite. These vows involved these three things, (1) abstinence from wine and strong drink, (2) refraining from cutting the hair off the head during the whole period of the continuance of the vow, and (3) the avoidance of contact with the dead.

In a mocking attempt to heap more ridicule on the enemies of Israel, Samson posed a riddle that he knew his Philistine enemies could never answer, even given the seven days of the wedding feast to resolve the riddle. The Philistines were so intent on winning this little contest with Samson that they enlisted his betrothed wife to entice the answer from him on threat of death to both her and her family (see Judg. 14:15).

Samson's wife wept on him and said, "You only hate me! You do not love me! You have posed a riddle to the sons of my people, but you have not explained it to me" (Judges 14:16).

A deceptive spirit has been released against the Lord's anointed that has been identified as the snare of the "Jezebel spirit." This spirit comes against the life of anointed men and women of God in an attempt to entice and allure them away from their God-given calling and destiny. The Jezebel spirit is *not* gender specific. It is gender neutral. Anyone can be under the influence of and operating in the power of the Jezebel spirit. Samson, as a Nazarite, was never to let wine touch his lips, and he was never to cut his hair. He was to live a sanctified life, separated unto God. But Samson allowed mixture in his life. He was enticed by the things of this world; the lust of the flesh, the lust of the eyes, and the pride of life. Because of this, he opened the door to becoming ensnared by the enemy, and this Jezebel spirit began to manipulate him and caused him to compromise to an even greater extent.

He said to his wife, "Look I have not explained it to my father or to my mother, so should I explain it to you?" Now she wept on him seven days while their feast lasted and it happened on the seventh day that he told her because she pressed him so much. Then she explained the riddle to the sons of her people. So the men of the city said to him on the seventh day before the sun went down: "What is sweeter than honey? And what is stronger than a lion?" And he said to them, "If you had not plowed with my heifer, you would have not solved my riddle." Then the Spirit of the Lord came upon him mightily, and he went down to Ashkelon and killed 30 of their men, took their apparel and gave the changes of clothing to those who had explained the riddle. So his anger was aroused, and then he went back up to his father's house and Samson's wife was given to his companion who had been his best man (Judges 14:16-20).

Christ Rather Than Compromise

The parallels and prophetic significance for this Seventh Day are evident. For 6,000 years or six days we have allowed compromise in our midst. We have embraced a mixture of spirit and flesh or God and the world and we have endorsed it as being "God." This mixture in our lives, this lack of separation and consecration, has influenced us to the point of almost becoming ineffectual in ministry and in modeling true Christ-like character to a lost and dying world. We are never going to fulfill the destiny of God for our lives if we continue to allow this mixture in our life. Where mixture is allowed, there will be leaven, and it will contaminate the whole loaf, whether for good or for evil. We have a choice to make on this Seventh Day. The attempts of this Jezebel spirit are growing more intense and insistent as the end of this age draws near. With the full force of its persuasive power coming to bear upon this generation, it will try and cause us to commit the ultimate compromise—rejection and betrayal of the Lord.

However, on the Seventh Day there is an anointing that is available to the people of God who have made the decision to stand for righteousness; those who have made the decision to be holy and separate unto God; those who have made the decision to walk in purity and the fear of the Lord—this generation of committed overcomers will rise up and destroy the works of the flesh and will remove the mixture from their midst and say, "No! We choose to be separate and holy unto God! That thing that past generations have been entangled with, that thing that we were going to be married to; that mixture of the world and the Spirit, we are not going to settle for that anymore!"

The Lord is releasing an aspect of the seven spirits of God upon this generation in a new and unique way. It is the Spirit of Might, the same spirit that was upon Samson, that will no longer tolerate compromise and will no longer accommodate the works of the flesh, the lust of the eyes, and the pride of life. It will be realized through a radical, violent, taking the Kingdom of God by force type of spirit that is going to say, *"no more mixture!* We will be separate! We will not allow the world access into our lives and into our family any longer." This walk is not for the feeble-hearted. It will be a very difficult walk because so much carnality and compromise has been prevalent in the Church that it has become the norm. And because it has been the norm, anything that is not modeled along the same lines will be considered either reactionary or revolutionary. As we choose and allow this sanctification process, we will become a whole different class of believers, unrecognizable to this carnal and lukewarm generation as the same Christians they have always known and been accustomed to. We will model the Kingdom of Heaven on earth with *power*.

Preparing His Bride

The Lord is going to receive unto Himself, in this Seventh Day, a bride that is prepared and ready. I was always taught in Bible College and in most of the churches I attended over the years, that the Church was the bride. I also had a good friend of mine who has since gone to be with the Lord who said, "No, the bride is the city." That is right in part. You are called Zion, the city of God.

The Holy Spirit challenged my theology regarding the Bride of Christ one day saying, "Who is the bride? Is the Church the bride?"

I said "Yes, Lord, that is what I learned in Bible College."

And He said, "No, that isn't correct."

So I said, "What do you mean Lord?"

He said, "Turn to Genesis 1, and I will teach you something."

When God created Adam He said that it was not good for man to be alone and the Lord put Adam into a deep sleep. While in this state of sleep, the Lord created from a rib out of Adam's side his help mate, Eve. He did not say in Genesis 1 that Adam was cloned and Eve "became." He said Eve came "Out of the side of the first Adam." (See Genesis 2:18-23.)

Now remember the Law of First Mention. When we talk about the bride of Christ, we can interpret the Scripture based upon "first mention." Jesus Christ is the second Adam who was the personification and fulfillment of every Old Testament type. Just as Eve came out of the side of Adam so *out of the body* of Christ comes the bride. Jesus will not be cloned.

In Genesis chapter 24, Abraham, who is a type of God the Father, sent his servant back to his family to find a bride for his son Isaac, who is a type of Christ. We see a picture of an end-time wedding feast that is being prepared. A bride is coming forth. So we have a type of God the Father, Abraham, who sends his helper Eleazar, a type of the Holy Spirit, into the world to find a bride for his son, Isaac. So the servant goes back to Abraham's family and from his family he receives a bride for Isaac and brings her to her bridegroom. Notice, the whole family did not become the bride! It was Rebecca alone who passed the test that the servant arranged and who was qualified to become the bride.

To date, the mixtures we have allowed in our lives have almost disqualified us. The Scripture says, however, that the Lord is going to come back for a Church without spot or blemish. In doing so, He has given us an opportunity to become this bride (see Eph. 5:27). Look at Revelation 19:7-8:

> *Let us be glad and rejoice and give Him glory, for the marriage*
> *of the Lamb has come, and His wife has made herself ready. And*
> *to her it was granted to be arrayed in fine linen, clean and*
> *bright, for the fine linen is the righteous acts of the saints.*

A Holy Invitation

To her it was granted—an invitation was extended. Salvation for all of us is a free gift. The infilling of the Holy Spirit is a free gift. The gifts of the Spirit enumerated in First Corinthians 12 through 14 are free gifts. But to become the Bride of Christ is by invitation; it is granted unto you to "become" this bride, yet it is conditional. Revelation 19:8 says, "*To her it was granted to be arrayed in fine linen.*" According to the history and culture of the day, *fine linen* speaks of the righteous man exhibiting to the eye of faith "the glory as of the only begotten of the Father, full of grace and truth" (John 1:14). It was also a symbol of cleanliness. Because of its light weight, the wearer would not sweat as much from daily exertions. On the priest, this symbolized the fact that it was not the sweat of the human's brow that brought about atonement, but the sacrifice of a pure heart, one who was at rest with his or her God.

The significance of this for the Seventh Day and an end-time generation is simply this: Nothing we can do in our own strength will qualify us to become part of the Bridal Company of Believers but this: "*It was granted* [to her] *to be arrayed in fine linen, clean and bright for the fine linen is the righteous act of the saints*" (Rev. 19:8).

Only speak when spoken through and only do what He tells you to do! Prepare yourselves; be armed and ready for warfare. How? By immersing yourself in God's Word and in the God of the Word; by being instant in season and out, and by going and doing exactly what He says without doubt, without hesitation, without question. By remaining in *rest*—a ceasing from our own works and a total reliance upon the Holy Spirit.

Sin in the Camp

We will never get there without relationship! There are so many stories I've heard that are comical, but at the same time they show acts of obedience that are profound. We have told the story about a good friend of ours who was ministering in a church one day, and the Lord said, "Speak and say, 'There is sin in the camp.'"

He said, "Lord, I can't do that. I'll never be asked back here again."

The Lord said again, "Speak and say there is sin in the camp, and this is what it is: The pastor's wife and the associate pastor's wife are having an affair."

He said, "Lord I can't say that, I'll never be invited back..."

Finally he just said, "Yes, Lord." And when he spoke it out, you could have heard a pin drop. He was convinced he had missed the Lord and that his ministry was over, but all of a sudden the pastors' wives began to weep. Brokenness and repentance came that caused a move of God. We must truly know God, intimately and personally in this hour!

Another minister was in Germany at a large banquet meeting. After the meal he was speaking, and there was a man back in the corner at a table sitting with his wife, looking very uncomfortable and unreceptive.

The Lord said, "I want you to do something. Go back, nibble on that man's ear, and tell him that I love him."

This brother argued with God a little bit (OK, a whole lot!) but finally said, "Okay, Lord."

He went back and said, "Sir, I have a word for you from the Lord."

The man said, "What?" So this brother leaned over, nibbled on his ear, and said, "Jesus loves you."

The man immediately broke down and began weeping. The story was that for some years this man's wife had been sharing the Gospel with her husband in hopes of his salvation. She would always ask and even plead with him saying, "Come to church; come to church."

Finally he said, "Look, I'll come to this banquet if you will stop bothering me." They had been married for a number of years and every night as they would fall off to sleep his wife would nibble his ear and say, "Honey, I love you."

So, thinking he could outmaneuver the Lord, he said, "If God is real, He is going to have to nibble on my ear and tell me He loves me."

That night a soul was brought into the Kingdom through radical obedience. Faith wasn't operative because of the absence of doubt in either of these cases, trust me. Yet obedience won out; faith won out.

Of No Reputation

Too often, we are worried about our reputation. I cannot tell you the number of times I have been cautioned to guard my reputation. While that has some merit when it comes to walking in Christ-like character, it has nothing to do with obedience. If I am walking in obedience to the Lord, then I am dead, and my life is hidden in Christ. I do not have to worry about looking foolish in the eyes of humankind. It is no longer I who live, but Christ who lives in me, and the life I now live I live by the faith of the Son of God! (see Gal. 2:20).

We cannot measure ourselves by the world's standards. We cannot have mixture in our hearts and in our lives. We cannot be married to the world and married to God. We can be the Bride of Christ, but we have to weave a garment, and that garment consists of the righteous acts of the saints. *"Faith without works is dead"* (James 2:20).

In the community where I live, we have an abundance of wildlife. Deer, elk, bear, and so forth roam the wilds here. Unfortunately, because of the abundance of game, it isn't uncommon to have vehicular deer strikes leaving dead and decaying carcasses along the road. In the summer heat, the odor of death and decay is overpowering. It stinks! I believe with all my heart, in the realm of the Spirit, there is scent, resonance, texture, frequency, color, and taste that can be discerned as we learn to be led of the spirit of God and to exercise our spiritual senses. *"Faith without works is dead"* (James 2:26). As I've stated above, when something is dead, it stinks!

Remember the question we used to ask as new believers, "Can the devil read your mind?" (I thought, "Well, if he could, it would be a short story.") In the realm of the spirit, when you walk in unbelief and disobedience; when you are outside of rest and you habitually wallow in these things, a fragrance is released in the realm of the spirit. If you are in faith, it will be a sweet-smelling savor to the Lord. However, if we are open to sin, the fragrance is a repugnant stench that draws demons from miles around. It is like a magnet or like flies to a kill.

The Righteous Bride

Not only does the Bride of Christ weave a wedding garment consisting of the righteous acts of the saints, but she releases a sweet-smelling fragrance by those very same acts of obedience. To us, it has been granted to become.

In Second Samuel 11:1-27 we have the story of David and Bathsheba. Rather than going out to war with his armies, David remained in Jerusalem during their war with the people of Ammon. During a sleepless night, David took a walk on the roof of his home, and he saw a woman bathing in her house. He let his eyes wander where they should not have wandered, which allowed sin to be conceived in his heart—which, in turn, caused him to do things he should not have done. He *should* have been off to war fighting the battles of God. But instead he stayed at home, and because he was not in the will of God or in the place that God wanted him in at that time, his eyes wandered and he was captured by his own lust. Idleness opened the door for the fruit of disobedience to bring forth fruit…lust.

David's Judgment

In Second Samuel 12:1-25, we see the response of God to David's sin:

Then the Lord sent Nathan to David. And he came to him, and said to him: "There were two men in one city, one rich and the other poor. The rich man had exceedingly many flocks and herds. But the poor man had nothing, except one little ewe lamb which he had bought and nourished; and it grew up together with him and with his children. It ate of his own food and drank from his own cup and lay in his bosom; and it was like a daughter to him. And a traveler came to the rich man, who refused to take from his own flock and from his own herd to prepare one for the wayfaring man who had come to him; but he took the poor man's lamb and prepared it for the man who had come to him." So David's anger was greatly aroused against the man, and he said to Nathan, "As the Lord lives, the man who has done this shall surely die! And he shall restore fourfold for the lamb, because he did this thing and because he had no pity." Then Nathan said to David, "You are the man! Thus says the Lord God of Israel: 'I anointed you king over Israel, and I delivered you from the hand of Saul. I gave you your master's house and your master's wives into your keeping, and gave you the house of Israel and Judah. And if that had been too little, I also would have given you much more! Why have you despised the commandment of the Lord, to do evil in His sight? You have killed Uriah the Hittite with the sword; you have taken his wife to be your wife, and have killed him with the sword of the people of Ammon. Now therefore, the sword shall never depart from your house, because you have despised Me, and have taken the wife of Uriah the Hittite to be your wife.' Thus says the Lord: 'Behold, I will raise up adversity against you from your own house; and I will take your wives before your eyes and give them to your neighbor, and he shall lie with your wives in the sight of this sun. For you did it secretly, but I will do this thing before all Israel, before the sun.'" So David said to Nathan, "I have sinned against the Lord." And Nathan said to David, "The Lord also has put away your sin; you shall not die. However, because by this deed you have given great occasion to the enemies of the Lord to blaspheme, the child also who is born to you shall surely die." Then Nathan departed to his house. And the Lord struck the child that Uriah's wife bore to David, and it became ill. David therefore pleaded with God for the child, and David fasted and went in and lay all night on the ground. So the elders of his house arose and went to him, to raise him up from the ground. But he would not, nor did he eat food with them. Then on the seventh day it came to pass that the child died. And the servants of David were afraid to tell him that the child was dead. For they said, "Indeed, while the child was alive, we spoke to him, and he would not heed our voice. How can we tell him that the child is dead? He may do some harm!" When David saw that his servants were whispering, David perceived that the child was dead. Therefore David said to his servants, "Is the child dead?" And they said, "He is dead." So David arose from the ground, washed and anointed himself, and changed his clothes; and he went into the house of the Lord and worshiped. Then he went to his own house; and when he requested, they set food before him, and he ate. Then his servants said to him, "What is this that you have done? You fasted and wept for the child while he was alive, but when the child died, you arose and ate food." And he said, "While the child was alive, I fasted and wept; for I said, 'Who can tell whether the Lord will be gracious to me, that the child may live?' But now he is dead; why should I fast? Can I bring him back again? I shall go to him, but he shall not return to me." Then David comforted Bathsheba his wife, and went in to her and lay with her. So she bore a son, and he called his name Solomon. Now the Lord loved him, and He sent word by the hand of Nathan the prophet: So he called his name Jedidiah, because of the Lord.

Nathan was sent by the Lord to confront David, and he did so by telling him a parable. *"There were two men in one city, and there was a rich man and a poor man..."* (see 2 Sam. 12:1). Nathan revealed the sin of David's heart, but David, blinded by lust and self-righteousness, totally missed the point of the parable.

The story continues: *"So David's anger was greatly aroused against the man, and he said to Nathan, 'As the Lord lives, the man who has done this shall surely die, and he shall restore fourfold for the lamb"* (2 Sam. 12:5-6). David's anger was aroused toward the man Nathan told him about who did this thing, and David has no pity for the man's actions.

Ministry of Reconciliation

We can learn something from this as Christians. Often the judgment that we face in this life for the things we do will come out of our own mouths. Scripture says, *"Judge not lest you be judged, for with the same judgment you judge you shall be judged"* (see Matthew 7:1). This is why we are admonished to be quick to listen, slow to speak, and slow to anger (see James 1:19). When we see sin in the camp and leaders falling and sin being exposed in the Body of Christ, the very first thing we should do is fall on our knees and repent saying, "God forgive *us*. Help *us*." Why? *We* are the Body of Christ. If a ministry falls into ineffectiveness because of sin, we must realize that we have been diminished to the extent that person's effectiveness has been negated. We need each member of the Body of Christ to be whole and functioning in its sphere of ministry.

All of us have been called to a ministry of reconciliation and restoration. We have not been called to a ministry of stone throwing and mockery. We need to restore that one in the spirit of meekness. Unfortunately, that is not human nature or even normal church culture. Yet that is the measure of the stature of Christ we of this Seventh Day must embrace and emulate. Anything less than a heart of repentance and brokenness on behalf of fallen brothers and sisters is childishness and immaturity. It is not the spirit of Christ, and it is not the heart of the Father.

So David pronounced judgment upon himself out of his own mouth. In Second Samuel 12:7-14 we read,

> *Nathan said to David, 'You are the man! Thus says the Lord God of Israel, 'I anointed you King over Israel, and I delivered you from the hand of Saul. I gave you your master's house and your master's wives into your arms, and gave you the house of Israel and Judah. If all of this had been too little, I also would have given you much more!' Why did you despise the commandment of the Lord to do evil in his sight? You have killed Uriah the Hittite with your sword, you have*

taken his wife to be your wife, and you have killed him with the sword of the people of Ammon. Now therefore the sword shall never depart from your house as you have despised me, and have taken the wife of Uriah the Hittite to be your wife. Thus says the Lord: 'Behold, I will raise up adversity against you from your own house; and I will take your wives before your eyes and give them to your neighbor, and he shall lie with your wives in the sight of this sun. For you did it secretly, but I will do this thing before all Israel, before the sun.' So David said to Nathan, "I have sinned against the Lord." And Nathan said to David, "The Lord also has put away your sin; you shall not die. However, because by this deed you have given great occasion to the enemies of the Lord to blaspheme, the child also who is born to you shall surely die."

Notice the sin was considered to be against the Lord as despising Him! Yes, there was a sin committed against Uriah and against his wife, but ultimately David sinned against the Lord. Though we may sin against our brothers and sisters, ultimately we have sinned against the Lord by despising the provision of the covenant we have with Him. Although, oftentimes, we unknowingly transgress and despise the Lord by our words and our actions, there is a day which is unlike any other day where we will see the maturation of the Body of Christ whose passion and purpose will be to honor the King of Glory in all they say and in all they do; that day is this Seventh Day!

Now David did something that we should all learn to do, and do immediately, when sin is exposed in our lives. He fell on his face and repented, and said, "God forgive me, I'm wrong." He didn't try and justify himself. He didn't make excuses, he just said, "I am wrong, I repent." We see something happening here on this Seventh Day that we need to learn. Individually and corporately, we must learn to take responsibility for our words and actions. What started with

Adam's excuse of, "Lord, the woman you gave me" (see Gen. 3:12) must end with a heart of humility saying, "Father, forgive me."

Do not try and take the pre-eminence and become a leader before God releases you. The judgment on a leader is far greater because leaders affect the lives of multitudes.

Second Samuel 12:15-18 says, *"And the Lord struck the child that Uriah's wife bore to David and it became ill. David therefore pleaded with God for the child's life and he fasted and went and lay all night on the ground. So the elders of the Church arose and went to him to raise him up from the ground, but he would not, nor did he eat food with them. Then on the seventh day it came to pass that the child died, and the servants of David were afraid to tell him that the child was dead. For they said, "indeed when the child was alive we spoke to him, and he would not heed our voice. How can we tell him that the child is dead, he may do some harm."*

A Church Without Blemish

Let this sink deeply into your heart. That which is birthed out of sin and rebellion will not fulfill or accomplish the purposes of God on earth. What originates from sin will die. It will not carry the presence of God or the anointing of God. Though there may be a repentant heart (as David displayed) and perhaps even fasting and interceding, that which is birthed out of rebellion is doomed to failure! God does not bless sin nor does He bless the fruit of sin.

It is the Seventh Day. As this millennium unfolds, we are going to see churches and ministries, those things that were birthed in sin and rebellion, die. They will not be used to fulfill the purposes of God in the earth. The day of mixture being overlooked is over. Jesus is coming back for a Church without spot or blemish. Anything birthed in sin is not going to have the Spirit of

God operative in it. At best it will be a false anointing leading the unaware deeper in to lethargy and acceptance of doctrines of demons. Churches or movements birthed in sin will produce compromise in its adherents and carnality in everything it does.

Second Samuel 12:19 says, *"When David saw that his servants were whispering...."* We see a picture here of servants who are afraid to speak the truth. They will not say that what David was trying to do was not going to work! "Pastor, it is going to die. This thing isn't of God." We need men and women of courage today who will speak the truth in love. As leaders, we need to surround ourselves with men and women of courage who will help us to keep accountable to the Word of God and the God of the Word. When pastors or leaders consider themselves above correction, they are not pastors or leaders; they are dictators.

> *David perceived that the child was dead. Therefore David said to his servants, "Is the child dead?" And they said, "He is dead." So David arose from the ground, washed and anointed himself, and changed his clothes; and he went into the house of the Lord and worshiped. Then he went to his own house; and when he requested, they set food before him, and he ate. Then his servants said to him, "What is this that you have done? You fasted and wept for the child while he was alive, but when the child died, you arose and ate food." And he said, "While the child was alive, I fasted and wept; for I said, 'Who can tell whether the Lord will be gracious to me, that the child may live?' But now he is dead; why should I fast? Can I bring him back again? I shall go to him, but he shall not return to me."* (2 Samuel 12:19-23)

There are things that were not conceived in righteousness that the Lord will remove from our lives on this day. They have been distractions, birthed of the flesh, and not conducive to the fulfillment of the destiny of God in our life. We have an opportunity, an unprecedented opportunity today to allow the Spirit of God to convict us of sin, deal with issues in our lives, and remove from us the works of the flesh.

As we allow Him to expose these things in our lives, we have an opportunity to respond in a redeeming way. Just as David did, we can arise, receive a fresh anointing, and repent of our foolishness and sin.

We must make room for a different mind-set on this day. If our plans don't seem to be working out, perhaps it is time for us to ascertain whether or not they are *our* plans or His plans. Understand that His plans will always work out if we yield to Him.

CHAPTER 8

Harvest and Power

On the Seventh day when the heart of the king was merry with wine, he commanded...seven eunuchs...bring Queen Vashti before the king, wearing her royal crown, in order to show her beauty to the people... But Queen Vashti refused (Esther 1:10-12).

Just as Vashti was invited to a banquet, so we have all been invited to a wedding feast. In Matthew 22:1-13, it says that a wedding feast was prepared, but because those invited refused to come, God said, *"Go to the highways and the byways and find as many as you can"* (see Matt. 22:9). You can also refuse to be part of the bridal company of believers. You can refuse the command of the King, and disqualify yourself from what God is saying today. Because of Queen Vashti's refusal to be obedient to the king, she was replaced with Esther.

I believe we are in a season of a changing of the guard. Some are graduating and going home, some are digging in their heels and refusing to let go of the past paradigm of the sixth day; yet we also see a remnant company of believers coming forth in this hour who are fully embracing the new stratagems of Heaven for this season. The Lord is doing a new thing on this day. It has never been seen before, and it has never been experienced before. It will cause us to reexamine our understanding of *church* and move us from inactivity to consistent works of faith as progress, further into this day.

> *And it came to pass in the eleventh year, in the first month, on the seventh day of the month, that the word of the Lord came to me, saying, "Son of man, I have broken the arm of Pharaoh king of Egypt; and see, it has not been bandaged for healing, nor a splint put on to bind it, to make it strong enough to hold a sword. Therefore thus says the Lord God: 'Surely I am against Pharaoh king of Egypt, and will break his arms, both the strong one and the one that was broken; and I will make the sword fall out of his hand* (Ezekiel 30:20-22).

In studying Scripture allegorically, we sometimes discover deeper truths that are not as obvious as those we find any other way. The king of Egypt and Egypt itself are examples. Egypt is a type of the world. Satan is a type of Pharaoh, the ruler of this world. On this Seventh Day the Lord has broken satan's arm, or limited his ability to wreck havoc upon the Kingdom of God. He will be ineffective in his warfare and schemes against us as we learn to trust in God, heed His voice, and do as He commands.

A new day is dawning, a new season that will witness the release of a new strategy for effective spiritual warfare that will render the enemy ineffective against us in our obedience to God. This is the strategy: The Lord will fight for you. A people of rest—a people who have ceased from their own works and no longer strive in their own strength—will see the Lord move in their behalf exceedingly abundantly above all they could ask or think! (See Ephesians 3:20.)

> *Then the hand of the Lord was upon me there, and He said to me, "Arise, go out into the plain, and there I shall talk with you."* (Ezekiel 3:22).

Who did it? God did it! It was not the Church with her programs and platitudes. It was not the covenant people of God speaking the Word as a formula. It was the Lord Himself who spoke and rendered the king of Egypt harmless to His people. Get this in your heart. God Himself is going to fight our battles for us as we are obedient to Him, and we will stand and see the salvation of God.

The Coming of the King

Thus says the Lord God: "The gateway of the inner court that faces toward the east shall be shut the six working days; but on the Sabbath it shall be opened, and on the day of the New Moon it shall be opened.

The prince shall enter by way of the vestibule of the gateway from the outside, and stand by the gatepost. The priests shall prepare his burnt offering and his peace offerings. He shall worship at the threshold of the gate. Then he shall go out, but the gate shall not be shut until evening.

Likewise the people of the land shall worship at the entrance to this gateway before the Lord on the Sabbaths and the New Moons.

The burnt offering that the prince offers to the Lord on the Sabbath day shall be six lambs without blemish, and a ram without blemish;

And the grain offering shall be one ephah for a ram, and the grain offering for the lambs, as much as he wants to give, as well as a hin of oil with every ephah.

On the day of the New Moon it shall be a young bull without blemish, six lambs, and a ram; they shall be without blemish.

He shall prepare a grain offering of an ephah for a bull, an ephah for a ram, as much as he wants to give for the lambs, and a hin of oil with every ephah.

When the prince enters, he shall go in by way of the vestibule of the gateway, and go out the same way (Ezekiel 46:1-8).

We know the eastern gate into the city of Jerusalem has been sealed and shut because there were prophecies saying the King of Glory, Jesus, was going to come through the eastern gate. The ancients thought, *Not only are we going to seal it shut, but we are going to put a grave here.* According to Jewish law, you cannot step on the grave of a dead person, otherwise you are unclean. In placing the graves of the dead there, the enemies of Israel think they will thwart the prophecy of the King of Glory entering by way of the eastern gate.

What they failed to take into account is that Jehovah is almighty, and He already has a strategy in place. The dead are going to rise, and the gate is going to be opened. This will take place on the Seventh Day, the Sabbath. The gate shall be opened and the Prince shall enter by the way of the vestibule of that gateway from the outside. Jesus, The Prince of Peace, is going to enter through this gate on the Seventh Day and He is going to come through in triumph. He is going to come through as the Prince of Peace and the Ruler of this world. He is going to establish his millennial Kingdom, and when He establishes His throne, the Rivers of Life will flow out through this eastern gate down into the Dead Sea. This is that day! His final triumphal entry is about to take place and you and I are positioned to have a front row seat!

As previously mentioned, today there are people having encounters with a resurrected Christ in visions, dreams, and many different ways, and millions of people across the world are coming to a saving knowledge of Christ as a result. Earlier, we mentioned that Muslims are having visitations of the Lord. These things are happening in the Middle East in Israel and Arabia and literally all over the world. The Lord is moving in unprecedented ways and He is doing extraordinary things. The question that remains to be answered then is, *Why is the Lord doing this in this season at this time?*

In Acts 1:11 we read, *Men of Galilee, why do you stand gazing up into heaven? This same Jesus, who was taken up from you into heaven, will so come in like manner as you saw Him go into heaven.*

From resurrection morning or early in the morning of the third day, until 40 days later in Bethany at His ascension, Jesus appeared to virtually 90 percent of the known Church in resurrected bodily form. First Corinthians 15 says He appeared to, "Upwards of five hundred people at one time" (see 1 Cor. 15:6). He also appeared to the disciples and the ladies of the tomb.

Jesus said that in the same way that He left, He is coming again. One of the clearest signs to this generation that the return of Christ is soon to take place is this particular passage of Scripture, coupled with the multiplicity of visions and encounters with the resurrected Jesus Christ. Of those whom we have encountered that have this testimony, every single one of them had this in common: the message that Jesus was coming sooner than anyone expects.

The Enoch Generation

Jude 14 says that Enoch was the seventh from Adam. We are the Seventh Day (the seventh millennium) removed from Adam! We are an end-time Enoch generation. We are a generation that will not have to taste of death, but we are going to have an encounter with God that is going to cause us in a moment, in the twinkling of an eye, to be changed and transformed. I am not resigned to physical death and then eternal life. I look forward to supernatural translation into Heaven. That may be too radical for some people, but I want to provoke people to start digging into the Word and to getting revelation for this hour instead of sitting back on their blessed assurance, biding their time until Jesus comes back.

> *At that time Jesus went through the grain fields on the Sabbath* [of the Seventh Day]. *And His disciples were hungry, and began to pluck heads of grain and to eat* (Matthew 12:1).

> *The Word says, "Don't tell me it is four months to the harvest, I tell you the fields are ripe unto harvest."* (See John 4:35 NKJV.)

What is the harvest? The harvest at the end of the age, the Seventh Day, is souls. However, on this day, the Sabbath Day, Jesus and the disciples are harvesting. That is why we are constantly hearing testimonies of people having an encounter with Jesus. This is the Seventh Day. We should be of desperate hunger and passion—a people so desperate for the return of Christ that we are actively working in the harvest fields and plucking the grain to fulfill the desire of the Lord's heart—the salvation of the lost.

We know scripturally that everything we set our hand to, as we are obedient to God, He is right there working with us. In fact, He says that He goes before us and He makes a way where there seems to be no way. Something about this day stands uniquely and intrinsically apart from all previous days and seasons. There is something about the communion of the Holy Spirit, the linking together of arms with God the Father, and working and walking and doing what He says to do on this day that transcends every other day. Ministry has never been so fruitful and in its own way, easy. I don't mean that in a trite way. I mean the Lord is doing something unique in the earth today. God's heart, His passion, is to see this thing finished. He wants you home! He is desperate for you! He desires for you to become everything He says you are and to have you model Heaven on earth. He has been waiting for six days.

In Matthew 12:2 it says, *"The Pharisees saw it and they said, 'Your disciples are doing what is not lawful to do on the Sabbath!'"* As long as there are people, we are going to have Pharisees. Pharisees are those who diminish Scripture. Relegating it to second place, as reason, is more important to them than relationship. We are always going to have those who are saying the *now* Word of God is not relevant. Contrary to this stance, the Word of God can only be perceived by the Spirit of God, not by the intellect of humankind. Life comes through revelation of the Word.

Jesus Is the Word

We find a liberty in a life devoted to developing relationship with God that comes no other way. To be a friend of God transcends all other pursuits, both intellectually as well as in natural endeavors. I have found a principle in Acts chapter 9 that has been an inspiration for my walk with Christ from my earliest days as a newborn Christian until today. This principle is found in the conversion of Saul of Tarsus who later became Paul the apostle. During his encounter with the Lord, Saul asked two questions that showed me the order in which I should conduct my journey in Christ.

The first was, *"Who are you, Lord?"* (Acts 9:5). Our primary focus should be in developing relationship with the Lord. We must continually pursue the knowledge *of* God before we will ever walk in the God kind of knowledge.

The second question, then, forms the basis of my life and calling, established on the first question of relationship developed: *"Lord, what do you want me to do?"* (Acts 9:6). All true ministry will be the product of Christ-centered relationship.

The Lord provoked me with a question one day that challenged what I had been taught in Bible College and in the Church. I had been taught that the miracles of the Old Testament were pointing to Christ, and in Him all of these miracles saw their fulfillment. So under the new dispensation, we will never see the same type of miracles that occurred in the Old Testament. He asked, "Who did all those miracles in the Old Testament?"

My response was almost immediate, "You did, Lord."

He said, "That is correct; I did those miracles by releasing my Word. Jesus is the Word!"

And then He changed my theology and understanding by this statement. He said, *"The works that I do, you can do also"* (see John 14:12).

I thought, "Well, how about that!" Even though I had been told we would never see the same types of miracles in this day and age that we had seen in the Old Testament, it never set right in my spirit. The Scripture clearly teaches nothing is impossible to those who believe (see Matt. 17:20). Nothing! The Word says, *"Jesus Christ is the same yesterday, today and forever"* (Hebrews 13:8).

Communing in Heavenly Places

Being called as a prophet, I've always been a perceiver. I have always known when something was from God, many times without knowing why or how. I would just have a witness in my spirit man, and I would know. In my younger days as a Christian, I would oftentimes try to express what I knew was the Lord without being able to supply Scripture, and more times than not, I would catch flack for stating what I believed. After time, I became very circumspect in what I would speak and share, not because I didn't believe what I knew the Lord was saying, but because I was unable to communicate these perceptions biblically. I learned to respond to the Lord by stating, "Father, I believe you. I know I don't have to figure it out. But God, I need it from the Word so that I can convey to other people the truth of what you're saying."

That is one of the reasons I have such a passion for God's Word now. If I were to share with you some of the revelation the Lord has given me without the witness of the Word I would be construed as crazy. As it is, even with the foundation of the Word, there are times when people look at me askance because what the Lord is releasing in this hour is challenging to the comfortable gospel we've come to know and embrace—no matter how unscriptural it really is.

For instance, let me ask you a question: Can a person be in two places at one time?

According to the Word of God the answer is, yes, we can. In the study of quantum physics that type of intellectual question is not a problem, but as a Christian we balk at such a thing. Here is the truth as revealed by God's Word: *"But God, who is rich in mercy, because of His great love with which He loved us, even when we were dead in trespasses, made us alive together with Christ (by grace you have been saved), and raised us up together, and **made us sit together in the heavenly** places in Christ Jesus, that in the ages to come He might show the exceeding riches of His grace in His kindness toward us in Christ Jesus"* (Eph. 2:4-7).

We are already seated together with Him in heavenly places in Christ Jesus. So, can a man (or woman) be in two places at one time? The answer is yes.

In Matthew 12:3-5 we read, *"But He said to them, 'Have you not read what David did when he was hungry, he and*

*those who were with him: how he entered the house of God
and ate the showbread which was not lawful for him to eat,
nor for those who were with him, but only for the priests? Or
have you not read in the law that on the Sabbath the priests in
the temple profane the Sabbath, and are blameless?'"*

Bread of the Faces

On the Sabbath or the Seventh Day, David, a man after God's
own heart, did something that was considered unlawful. He entered the house of God and he ate the showbread (KJV shew-
bread). This passage intrigues me. Shew-bread is significant in its
prophetic implication for us today. Let me give you a definition
from Smith's Bible Dictionary:

Shew-bread, interpreted literally, is "bread of the face" or
"faces." Shew-bread was unleavened bread placed upon a table
which stood in the sanctuary together with the seven-branched
candlestick and the altar of incense. Every Sabbath, 12 newly
baked loaves, representing the 12 tribes of Israel, were put on the
table in two rows, six in each, and sprinkled with incense, where
they remained until the following Sabbath. Then, they were replaced by twelve new loaves, the incense was burned, and they
were eaten by the priests in the holy place, out of which they might
not be removed. The title "bread of the face" seems to indicate
bread through which God is seen, that is, with the participation of
which the seeing of God is bound up, or through the participation
of which man attains the sight of God. Hence, it follows that we
have not to think of bread merely as the means of nourishing the
bodily life, but as spiritual food and a means of appropriating and
retaining that life which consists of seeing the face of God.[1]

David entered the House of God on the Seventh Day and ate the
bread through which God is seen! Bread is significant allegorically

because it alludes to God's Word. The House of God, in context of what we have been studying and hearing, can mean either you and me as the temple of God, the temple in Israel (which no longer stands), or the third heaven where the Throne of God is.

If we take this to mean just the Body of Christ—you and me—as the temple, then we can see the significance of this revelation speaking to us on this Seventh Day. The Word of God, as we meditate and study it, will become *rhema* to us, causing us to be conformed to His image and character. We will realize the fullness of relationship with God—face to face, in an intimate way. This speaks of a generation that will be without spot or blemish at the return of Christ as we are changed from glory to glory—seeing Him.

The second aspect would be the fact that on the Sabbath, or the Seventh Day, David entered the House of God and ate this bread. As I shared earlier, multitudes today are having face-to-face encounters with the Lord, and many have had and are having third-heaven experiences—literally being caught up into the House of God.

In John 14:2, Jesus said, *"In my Father's house are many mansions. I go to prepare a place for you."*

The Bread of Life

The prophetic implication and possibility of God indicates that we can go into the House of God, from this realm to that, and eat the manna—the bread of life. The possibility of God right now is unlimited. I've often said this, and I believe it whole heartedly: The man with the experience is never at the mercy of the man with the theology. Now that does not mean I don't have to go to the Word to find Scripture and the truth of the Word for what has been experienced. We must test all things against Scripture, however, the truth is that theology (the study of God), many times, is based on human reasoning rather than revelation from God's Word, and so we keep ourselves from the life of God. The man with the godly experience is never at the mercy of the man with the theology.

We have a generation that says, "Prove to me that God is real." They have watched "Christianity," and the example they have had has been a lot of talk with no substance. Let's show them that God is real. Let's give them a tangible touch, an expression of the reality of what He has in store for them. As David did, let us lead the people into the House of God and feed them that "bread through which God is seen."

> Matthew 12:5-8 says, *Or have you not read in the law that on the Sabbath the priests in the temple profane the Sabbath, and are blameless? Yet I say to you that in this place there is One greater than the temple. But if you had known what this means, "I desire mercy and not sacrifice," you would not have condemned the guiltless. For the Son of Man is Lord even of the Sabbath.*

The Son of Man, Jesus, is Lord of the Sabbath. Jesus' Lordship, His authority, is going to be evident on the Seventh Day. As the Body of Christ advances toward a final clash with the forces of darkness we will discover an exponential understanding of the authority invested in us as sons of God. Unusual miracles are beginning to be displayed in contradistinction to the attempts of the prince of darkness's strategies to advance his malevolent intentions for humankind at the end of the age.

Operatively, what does *lordship* look like? It means wherever I stand, I have dominion and authority that I can exercise to expand the Kingdom of Heaven. It is going to be manifested in us and through us because we are coming to maturity in Jesus. We will comprehend and understand the fullness of the stature of the knowledge that has been imparted and invested in us. And where we walk, the Kingdom of Heaven is going to be released.

Sicknesses are going to flee. Diseases are going to flee. Demons are going to flee, and fear and doubt are going to flee. Everything will turn right side up as we began to walk in this revelation, in the supernatural endowment God is releasing for this generation. The fullness of the stature of what God intended for His creation to be, will be ours. This fullness and stature of the knowledge of God is going to be displayed in those who are willing to receive the Word of God and the revelation of God and yield to and be obedient to God.

> *When He had departed from there, He went into their synagogue* (Matthew 12:9).

> *So He came to Nazareth, where He had been brought up. And as His custom was, He went into the synagogue on the Sabbath day...* (Luke 4:16).

Divine Dissatisfaction

On the Seventh Day, the Sabbath, it was customary for Jesus to enter the temple. Some years ago, the Lord began to birth within the hearts of His people a greater hunger and passion for Him. It began as a subtle restlessness on the part of individuals who sensed that there was something more to their Christian walk than what they were currently experiencing. It progressed from there to what I call a "divine dissatisfaction" and has become a desperate cry for more. For almost two decades, this hunger has been increasing and leading to this moment, this season of destiny called the Seventh Day. It was the Lord who birthed within us this hunger and longing, and it is the Lord who is going to fulfill that desperate hunger in this hour by visiting His Temple on this Seventh Day!

Now when He had departed from there, He went into their synagogue. And behold, there was a man who had a withered hand. And they asked Him, saying, "Is it lawful to heal on the Sabbath?"—that they might accuse Him (Matthew 12:9-10).

There are many in Christendom who take the stance that healing is no longer for today, believing it ceased when the last apostle died. They might adhere to a doctrine, a theology, or a tradition that excludes the reality of the supernatural manifestations of the Spirit in our age, but the majority of those people are hungry for more of God, even if they don't know what that "more" is. The good news is Scripture says those who seek the truth, will find it. It doesn't matter if they are Buddhist, Hindu, Muslim, or Taoist. It doesn't matter if they are agnostic, atheist, Calvinist, Baptist, Charismatic, or whatever label we care to recognize. If there is a seed of hunger in you that desires truth, there has never been a better day for that desire to see fulfillment. Truth is going to be revealed.

Is it lawful to heal on this Seventh Day? Jesus asked them, *"What man is there among you who has one sheep, and if it falls into a pit on the* [seventh day] *will not lay hold of it, and lift it out?"* (Matt. 12:11). What is a sheep? Allegorically, we are the sheep of His pasture. Jesus asked, *"Of how much more value then is a man than a sheep? Therefore it is lawful"* (Matt. 12:12). Under this dispensation of grace, and especially on the Sabbath day, we are going to see the hand of God move in profound miracles of healing.

We are on the verge of a mighty outpouring of the Spirit of God that is unprecedented. The glory of this latter house shall be greater than the former (see Hag. 2:9). It has already begun. Astounding miracles are happening in many regions of the world, and we are just in the dawning of this day. We are witnessing an acceleration as we move further into this day of destiny, not only of miracles, but of their intensity and scope. The Lord has been speaking to many about a coming healing revival that will engulf the globe as part of a final witness and harvest. I believe we are going to see mass healings, mass deliverances, and mass encounters with the living God. Whole communities will be touched by the power of God and be healed, delivered, and set free spontaneously, as the Lord pours out His Spirit. We will see the raising of the dead on a scale never before experienced. There will be groups of people raised from the dead all at one time as the Lord demonstrates His power to this generation in extraordinary ways.

Then He said to the man, "Stretch out your hand." And he stretched it out, and it was restored as whole as the other (Matthew 12:13).

A Crisis of Faith

Now, we come to a crisis of faith. Everything this man had been taught by the religious system of his day screamed at him that this was not right! Even his leaders (pastors) said it was unlawful. He could have responded with, "No, we do it this way…This is what my denomination says. This is what my Bible College said, and that is what I have always believed," and the excuses go on. On this Seventh Day, the Lord is going to challenge us to step outside of our comfort zone and to move away from our pet doctrines and do something that we have never done before. He is going to ask us to trust Him completely and obey Him unreservedly.

Jesus commanded this man to do something contrary to all that he knew—stretch out your hand and be healed on this day. This man is faced with a life-altering decision. His question was, "Do I act contrary to everything I've known, even if it means I'm ostracized?" My question to you is, are you willing to be a friend of God and an enemy of the world; or would you rather compromise and be a friend of the world and an enemy of God and by doing so, remain in the halt and lame condition you have always been in?

We have a twofold revelation that speaks to us in regard to this Seventh Day. First, hands in Scripture symbolically speak of service. The picture we see is that of a man who is unable to serve God to the fullest extent of his God-given ability because he is hindered by the traditions and doctrines of men, rather than walking in liberty according to the Scripture (see Mark 7:5-8).

One of the signs of this Seventh Day that we will begin to see to a greater extent is the miracle of limbs being restored. It speaks both of the love and compassion of the Lord as well as depicting a release of God's people from the tyranny and bondage of man-made traditions that have hindered us from our destiny in God.

Jesus said to the man, *"Stretch out your hand."* As he responded in faith it was restored as whole as the other.

The second aspect of this revelation is this: Jesus, of His own volition, visited this particular temple and set this man free. He had been in this condition all of his life. He had resigned himself to being less than what he should have or could have been. The Scripture did not say he had been fasting and praying for this miracle. It did not say he had believed for this miracle. It was a divine act of love and compassion, a "suddenly" of God that invaded his life, and freedom was the result.

Do Give Away Your Miracle

There are many today who have given up on ever receiving their miracles of healing or release into the sphere of service the Lord has called them to. On this Seventh Day, multitudes who've been trapped in the tyranny of the familiar are going to have a "suddenly" encounter with the living God, and He is going to speak a Word of release over them. This is a day of completion! It is a day of every covenant promise being fulfilled! It is a day of rest—ceasing from our own works and allowing the Lord to release us to our destiny!

We cannot allow ourselves to be concerned with religious mind-sets and those who are following tradition rather than God when they decide to stand up and abuse, slander, or curse us. Remember, Pharaoh's arm is broken. Isaiah 54:17 says, "*No weapon formed against you shall prosper; and every tongue which rises against you…you shall condemn…*"

Liberty is coming to those who dare to believe God and do as He asks them to do, even when it may seem contrary to what they have always known as the norm. God's purposes will not be hindered or thwarted during this season of completion. We as a generation will hear the words, "It is finished" as the transition from the stewardship and rule of man is given to the King of kings and the Lord of lords. Just prior to this transition, we as a people of God will have every opportunity to enter in to the fullness of what we were created for. We will either be participating witnesses to the greatest move of God in all of recorded history, or we will remain where we are; on the bench as spectators in this final harvest. The decision as to whether you are a participant or spectator is yours.

ENDNOTE

1. William Smith & H.B. Hackett (ed.), *Dr. William Smith's Dictionary of the Bible*: 4 Volume Set (1889).

CHAPTER 9

Transformation

*And He said to them, "Assuredly, I say to you that there are some standing here who will not taste death till they see the kingdom of God present with power." Now **after six days** Jesus took Peter, James, and John, and led them up on a high mountain apart by themselves; and He was transfigured before them. His clothes became shining, exceedingly white, like snow, such as no launderer on earth can whiten them. And Elijah appeared to them with Moses, and they were talking with Jesus. Then Peter answered and said to Jesus, "Rabbi, it is good for us to be here; and let us make three tabernacles: one for You, one for Moses, and one for Elijah"— because he did not know what to say, for they were greatly afraid. And a cloud came and overshadowed them; and a voice came out of the cloud, saying, "This is My beloved Son. Hear Him!" (Mark 9:1-7).*

Jesus said to His disciples that there would be some of them who would not taste of death until they saw the Kingdom of God come in power. Then, *after* six days He took three of them up a high mountain with Him. After the sixth day comes the Seventh Day. On this Seventh Day, there are some who are going to see the Kingdom of God come in power! What exactly did Jesus mean when He told them they would see the Kingdom of God come in power? Verse 2 of Mark 9 gives us our clue. The word *transfigured* used here is the same word used in Hebrews 11:5 (KJV): "*By faith Enoch was translated* [transfigured]."

The aspect of the Kingdom of God that is coming in power on this Seventh Day is the transfiguration of the Body of Christ—when this mortal shall put on immortality! Death shall be done away and we, as Enoch, shall be caught away with Him to live in the presence of the Lord!

> *His clothes became shining, exceedingly white, like snow such as no launderer on earth can whiten them. And Elijah appeared to them with Moses, and they were talking with Jesus* (Mark 9:3-4).

There are many different facets of revelation in these two verses. First, we are the Body of Christ and Jesus said, "The works that I do, you can do also" (see John 14:12). (That alone, in conjunction with this passage of Scripture, is enough to excite us and jumpstart our faith!). Jesus went up to a high mountain and He began to interact with Heaven in a way never before seen or heard of. The glory of God so enveloped Him that He began to radiate that glory and He was literally able to communicate face to face with Elijah and Moses. We know that Moses had a similar experience, yet, he never talked to any of the patriarchs of old as Jesus was doing.

The Thin Places

Let me reiterate one more time: In Celtic Christianity, four or five hundred years ago, they would have certain places that they would use for intercession. They would spend days, weeks, months, and even years in intercession and worship to God. They did this so frequently that the place where they met became so permeated with the atmosphere of Heaven that it became a portal, an opening to Heaven. They called those places "thin places" because the fabric of reality was so thin that they could break through into the spirit realm almost instantly.

In the same way, your life can be a continual *thin place*. Remember the law of first mention? It states that the first time something is mentioned in Scripture, from that point on, every subsequent mention of the same subject may be interpreted by the first mention.

In Genesis 28:10-19, we read the story of Jacob's journey from Beersheba. As he is traveling, he stops for the night and he puts a stone under his head and goes to sleep. (I've stayed in the *rock-for-a-pillow* hotel a number of times in my travels!) During the night he has a dream in which the Lord communicates with him and he sees the angels of God ascending and descending a ladder that goes from earth to Heaven. When he awakens in the morning from his encounter with God, he makes a statement that is a first-mention in Scripture: Genesis 28:16-17, *"Then Jacob awoke from his sleep and said, "Surely the Lord is in this place, and I did not know it." And he was afraid and said, "How awesome is this place! This is none other than the house of God, and this is the gate of heaven!"*

Communicating in the Afterlife

"This is none other than the house of God, and this is the gate of heaven" (Gen. 28:17). First Corinthians 6:19 says *you* are the temple of God! As the house or temple of God, according to the Law of First Mention, you should be living continually under an open Heaven. You are a "gate" of Heaven. It should come as no shock to any believer that we can speak to the Lord face to face and see the angels of God ascending and descending from Heaven. *That* is normal Christianity! You are supposed to be a living, breathing, mobile example of a true *thin place*.

We need to redefine necromancy in light of this passage of Scripture in Mark chapter 9. Jesus was talking to Elijah and Moses, both of whom had gone on to be with the Lord. According to most definitions of *necromancy*, Jesus was interacting with the dead and so was in sin. The correct definition is this: "the practice of attempting to communicate with the spirits of the dead in order to predict or influence the future" or, "witchcraft or sorcery in general" (Encarta Dictionary).[1]

We know that Jesus was not practicing witchcraft, nor was he attempting to communicate with the spirits of the dead in order to predict the future. What He was doing was communicating with those who had gone from this earthly life to eternal life—they went from life to life. Only those who are *not* in covenant with the Lord, those who are *not* born-again, go from life to eternal death. Having contact with saints who have gone on to be with the Lord is not against Scripture. Trying to contact them of your own volition is.

When you leave this earth as a believer, you are not going from life to death; you are going from life to life. In Matthew 8:21, a young man came to Jesus and he said, "Lord let me first go and bury my father." Jesus responded, "No, let the dead bury the dead." *Leave the dead to bury their own dead* (see Matt. 8:22). The spiritually dead are always on hand to bury the physically dead, if one's real duty is with Jesus. Chrysostom says that, while it is a good deed to bury the dead, it is a better one to preach Christ.[2]

The Day of Transfiguration

The Church in Heaven and on the earth are one. Mark 9:3 says, *"His clothes became shining."* Remember the anointing of Paul was so great he would take handkerchiefs that he had worn on his body and he would hand them out and people would get healed. This happened with me in Fiji. Before Reshma and I were married

I was doing a conference in Suva, staying in a nice home of a family, and all the children had chicken pox. I caught a cold and had a fever that whole week, but I kept preaching. I knew the anointing would destroy the yoke of this chest cold. I kept going each evening to minister, but I was exhausted. I had such a bad fever, I would sweat all night in bed. Then the day I left, the mother took her four sick children and went up to the bed I had been sleeping in and rolled them in the bed, and they were instantly healed.

We are coming to a place on the Seventh Day of transfiguration and of translation. The best descriptive for this word is literally *rapture*. I don't mean the catching-away rapture. I mean being enraptured by God, immersed in God, so that even our clothes, our body, everything about us begins to shine forth the glory of God so that people can even see it.

In the story of the transfiguration, Peter was so taken by what he saw that he said, "*Rabbi, it is good for us to be here. Let us make three tabernacles; one for you, and one for Moses, and one for Elijah*" (Mark 9:5). We are beginning to witness a release of supernatural revelation knowledge coming to the Church on the Seventh Day. Just as Peter knew who Jesus was talking to by the spirit, we will know and gain knowledge, by a divine impartation of revelation, that no man or woman has ever taught or heard before. Our understanding will be enlightened.

"*And a cloud came and overshadowed them; and a voice came out of the cloud saying, "This is my beloved Son. Hear Him!*" (Mark 9:7). It's the Seventh Day! God the Father is saying, "You are my beloved son. World, hear him." We are in the season where the Body of Christ will come to the fullness of the stature of the knowledge of God, and of the God kind of knowledge! We are going to grow up into Him in *all* things! He said He is going to finish what He began, in us as well as in this world! The conclusion of the matter is at hand! Every promise will be fulfilled! We are a people called by His name, and there are going to be exploits done in His name that defy the imagination! We are going to be so immersed in God that we are going to look like God; we will act like God and we will talk like God! We are going to grow up to become everything He says we are! The heart of the Father is saying, "Look at them; they are my beloved."

> Mark 9:15 says, *Immediately, when they saw Him, all the people were greatly amazed, and running to Him, greeted Him.*

Why were they amazed? The glory of God was radiating off of Him that they were utterly astounded. They had never seen anything like this before!

Church, we are going to have a mountain-top experience with God and it is going to transform us and cause us to be conformed to the image of the One we love, and the One who loves us. People are going to look at us and be astounded. Why? They are going to see Jesus in us and upon us. We will be *"other than"* who you are right now, because the longing and the desire of our heart is going to be fulfilled.

> *Then they went into Capernaum, and immediately on the Sabbath He entered the synagogue and taught. And they were astonished at His teaching, for He taught them as one having authority, and not as the scribes. Now there was a man in their synagogue with an unclean spirit. And he cried out, saying, "Let us alone! What have we to do with You, Jesus of Nazareth? Did You come to destroy us? I know who You are—the Holy One of God!" But Jesus rebuked him, saying, "Be quiet, and come out of him!" And when the unclean spirit had convulsed him and cried out with a loud voice, he came out of him. Then they were all amazed, so that they questioned among themselves, saying, "What is this? What*

new doctrine is this? For with authority He commands even the unclean spirits, and they obey Him." And immediately His fame spread throughout all the region around Galilee (Mark 1:21-28).

Mark 1:21 says, "*Then they went into Capernaum, and immediately on the* [seventh day Jesus] *entered the synagogue.*" Early in the morning on the Seventh Day, immediately on the Seventh Day, God began to enter our life, enter our heart, enter His temple in a new and powerful way, and He began to teach us personally and to set us free. How is He doing that? He is doing it through His Word, anointed preaching and teaching, dreams, visions, and visitations. Immediately on the Sabbath day, Jesus is interacting with humankind, especially with His Church, right now, because you are going to become everything He says you are.

Jesus, the Word Himself, is coming to His temple, our hearts, in a unique and profound way! In other words, He is opening His Word, and giving us revelation and insight like we have never had before, and we are going to become *intimately* acquainted with Him! We are not going to just know *about* Him, but we are going to *know* Him! Our hearts, our character will be so fused together with His that the yearning of His heart will resound within our spirits as the loudest of commands! We will be so inseparable that people will think we are twins! That is what that word *know* signifies.

A River of Revelation

"*...And they were astonished at His teaching*" (Mark 1:22). I am profoundly astonished every time I open God's Word in this season as there seems to be an almost immediate download of revelation. A few years ago, Reshma and I were with Pastor John Rodham of Saint Luke's Episcopal in Ballard, Washington. This was the former

Church of Pastor Dennis Bennett who was considered one of the fathers of the Charismatic Movement, which began in the late 1960s.

Pastor John asked us, "Have you ever been in the old sanctuary where Dennis Bennett ministered?"

We answered, "No, we have never been there."

John said, "Well, just go on in there and stand upon the altar."

So we went and stood at the altar and looked at these beautiful stained glass windows behind the pulpit.

John said, "You guys are different; every single person that I have told to do that has gone up there and turned back around and faced this way [toward the pews]."

He then began to prophesy. He said, "I see you by the river of revelation. You're just frolicking like children on the bank of this river, splashing each other, and sometimes you jump in. The Lord says you're going to be living there, and everything you're going to do for the Kingdom will be from the banks of the river of revelation." Needless to say, we took that to heart and began to stand on this prophetic promise.

About two years later, I had a visitation of the Lord on Rosh Hashanah, and Jesus handed me a book. I said "Lord, what is this book?" I had been seeing this book in my spirit, both while awake and asleep off and on for nine months.

He said, "It's the *Book of Mysteries*; revelation that has been reserved for the end of the age." He said, "I'm releasing this to my Body in this fullness of time season."

My thoughts immediately went back to the prophetic word I had received from Pastor John a couple of years earlier. I thought, "Here's a book given called the *Book of Mysteries* and there is a river that is called the River of Revelation where we are going to be living. Lord, what exactly are you saying to us?"

About three weeks after this encounter we were ministering in Malaysia when a prophetess, a friend of ours, had a night free from ministry and came to hear us minister and to visit. After the meeting during dinner, she said, "This is really strange. I have to tell you this. Tonight I saw an angel standing by you, and I knew he had been assigned to your life. He is a new angel, and this is what God said: it is the angel that took John up on the mount above the New Jerusalem, and it is the angel of revelation. Did that make sense to you?"

I said, "Oh, yeah!"

Now I understood what it was the Lord was speaking. Let me explain something that is significant for all of us right now. When I began having visitations on Rosh Hashanah, the first thing the Lord said to me was that these experiences were not about me; they were indicative and prophetically speaking about this generation. In allowing me to have these experiences, I was to proclaim them to as many as I could to encourage them. This is about *you!* You have been called to live by this river of revelation. You have been handed a book—revelation reserved for this day. We all have access to these prophetic promises because the Lord said they are for this generation!

It's not about *me!* The Lord began weaning me away from that mentality many years ago. If He is speaking to me, He is speaking to many. If He is releasing to one, He is releasing many. He is releasing profound insight and revelation to His children in this generation.

The Wedding Feast

In the Book of John, chapter 2 we read about a wedding feast in Cana that took place on the third day (See my first book, *Prom-*

ise of the Third Day). The end of the story is new wine; the best wine, has been reserved for now! When is now? This third day and this Seventh Day. What is the wine? Revelation!

My father and I have had many discussions about churches praying for unity among themselves and others. I've come to this conclusion: we need to stop praying for unity and start praying for a revelation of Jesus in the lives of His people. Jesus is the great equalizer. We can continue to implement programs that may have some measure of success. But it will never be a lasting unity because people still have carnal ambitions and desires in their lives.

When you receive a revelation of Jesus, when you stand in the presence of the living God, then all of humankind's attempts and ambitions fade away into insignificance in the light of His Glory. Selfish ambition vanishes. The love of God is shed abroad in our hearts and we discover that unity is more a matter of relationship with God that reflects in our everyday relationships with each other.

The Lord is releasing to the Church on this Seventh Day an impartation of revelation, insight, and understanding that will allow us to model a supernatural unity founded upon the Love of God for our fellow man and woman. This unity will have no human attempts through programs or platitudes to conform to the Word, but it will be a supernatural work of grace at the end of the age. We will be *one new man* in Christ!

> *Now there was a man in their synagogue with an unclean spirit. And he cried out...* (Mark 1:23).

This is liberating. If you will recall in First Corinthians 6:19, we are called the temple of God. The prophetic Seventh Day picture we derive from this passage found in Mark 1:23 is this: within all of us there have been seasons of bondage where we have been ensnared by besetting sins that seemed to rule our lives. Some have fasted and prayed for freedom; some have gotten counsel; some have had others with healing or deliverance ministry pray for them, and yet there are still times when all of the above just doesn't seem to work.

On *this* Seventh Day, Jesus Himself, unbidden and sometimes not even expected, is visiting the synagogue (the temple), and He is initiating a deliverance and effecting a freedom from bondage that has held His people back from becoming whole! And those things that have held us in bondage, when the King of Glory comes in will be exposed for what they are, and we will be free to become the mature sons of God He has called us to be.

> *What have we to do with you, Jesus of Nazareth? Did you come to destroy us? I know who you are, the Holy One of God* (Mark 1:24).

Our inner man will bear witness with and recognize the holiness of God. That which is contrary to this spirit of holiness might go out screaming, but it *is* going to vacate the temple! It's time for us to be liberated from the snares of the devil as we fulfill the prophetic mandate established by God the Father before the foundation of the world: We will be a Church without spot or blemish, and we will be prepared at His coming!

I often jokingly make the statement that we can identify something quantifiable that is faster than the speed of light: darkness. When light comes in, darkness flees faster than the light coming in. The darkness that has ensnared us is about to be supernaturally eradicated by the presence of God being released within us. This is the beginning of our Mount of Transfiguration experience.

> *Immediately, His fame was spread abroad...* (Mark 1:28 KJV).

Power, Placement, and Preparation

Everything God does or has you to do on this Seventh Day is going to point to Him. If something occurs in the Church that is supernatural or awe-inspiring but we are told to focus on anything that points to a person, run away as fast as you can! The day of self adulation is over. The day of building our own kingdom (our ministry) is over. We are called to walk in humility and to build God's Kingdom. We are told to give Him glory. Anything other than this is idolatry.

> *Now as soon as they had come out of the synagogue, they entered the house of Simon and Andrew, with James and John. But Simon's wife's mother lay sick with a fever, and they told Him about her at once. So He came and took her by the hand and lifted her up, and immediately the fever left her. And she served them* (Mark 1:29-31).

Simon's mother-in-law lay sick with a fever. The first thing they did was take their concern to Jesus, and Jesus immediately went in unto her, took her by the hand and lifted her up. Hands in Scripture have great significance. The term *hand* can be associated with power in the hand, placement within boundaries, and preparation for ministry as well as service. Therefore, when Jesus took her by the hand, we see an amazing picture of power, placement, and preparation:

- *Power:* When Jesus placed His hand in her hand, power was released that set her free from the infirmity that had rendered her unable to function.

- *Placement:* By lifting her up, Jesus positioned her to function in her God-given gifting.

- *Preparation:* Now that she was healed and positioned, she was prepared to fulfill her ministry of service to those in her home.

In the same way that Jesus healed Peter's mother-in-law on the Sabbath, (Seventh Day), He is also visiting many of His covenant people and releasing power to restore them and placing them in the ranks of His end-time army. Upon His command, we are now prepared for service because we are healed and in position.

You will notice it was the intercession of Peter that brought his mother-in-law to Jesus' attention. Intercession on behalf of those who are unable to function in their full potential in the Body of Christ will see an effectiveness today that is unparalleled.

Mark 1:22 says, *They were astonished at His teaching, for He taught them as one having authority and not as the scribes.*

Jesus spoke from a position of relationship with the Father, while the scribes and Pharisees spoke from an interpretive standpoint based upon their limited ability to comprehend the Torah. Because of His relationship, Jesus spoke the truth, while corrupt, evasive, and reasoning religious spirits marked the sermons of the scribes and Pharisees. Friends, we are not here to appease flesh. We are here to crucify the flesh, expose flesh, and glorify God. If we try to pacify flesh, we are not sent of God.

We must be aware of a demarcation line between truth and error, good and evil, right and wrong. We cannot walk in holiness, purity, and the fear of God, and still allow fleshly attitudes and motivations to guide us. We cannot walk with God and be a friend of the world. Holiness is a separation from fleshly carnal desires. We can introduce no compromise to true holiness, and there can be no mixture. At the end of the age, this mixture is warned against as being symptomatic of those who are lukewarm.

Jesus presented matters of great significance: matters of life, death, and eternity, but the religious system of His day often wasted their time on trivialities. I learned a long time ago that it was not important to give you *just* a message *from the Bible* if it doesn't cause you to want to be more like Him. What is the point of that? What I consistently ask myself is this, "What am I doing to build Christ in those to whom I am ministering?" My passion is to see you change into the overcoming child of God you are called to be. Empty platitudes and powerless messages will not do that. I want to see fruit and character. I want to see Christ formed in us. If I'm not doing that, I may as well just go home and watch TV.

Confronting the Heart

Jesus always got to the heart of the matter by dealing with matters of the heart. Jesus said to the religious, to the Pharisees, *"Woe to you…hypocrites! For you shut up the kingdom of heaven against men; for you neither go in yourselves, nor do you allow those who are entering to go in…"* (Matt. 23:13). Today we have that same Gospel the Pharisees preached being carried out all over the earth in various denominational and doctrinal guises.

Jesus spoke as a lover of the souls of men, as one that was concerned with the everlasting welfare of his listeners, and He always pointed them to the Father and His love. The contrast between the Gospel of the Kingdom that Jesus shared and that of a religious system void of power is glaringly obvious, as seen in passages such as Mark 12:38-39. *"Beware of the scribes, who desire to go around in long robes, love greetings in the marketplaces, the best seats in the synagogues,* [and the accolades of men]…."

If people have to come and tell you how wonderful they are or what a great ministry they have, (i.e., Steve Stunning Evangelist or Prophet Profound), *run!* Don't walk, run! Get away! The fruit of Christ-like character is missing!

Now this is important: the Scripture specifically stated that Jesus spoke with authority (see Mark 1:22), for His message came straight from the very heart and the mind of the Father. It was revelation birthed out of relationship. The religious system of His day produced fallible concepts and interpretations of Scripture because rather than getting to know the Lord, one scribe would study the teachings of another and end up quoting another scribe. They were trying to draw water from broken cisterns, while He was drawing from within Himself, being a fountain of living water. When the children of Israel were in the wilderness, six days, they gathered manna, but on the Seventh Day they were *not* allowed to gather. You must have fresh manna every single day. I can't live on yesterday's revelation. I don't even want to. I love it, but I want more. The more He gives, the hungrier I get and the less I seem to know, because the Lord is such a vast reservoir of wisdom, understanding, knowledge, and insight that eternity will be required to even begin to discover Him! We are going to be discovering God for eternity, and if I'm content with yesterday's manna, yesterday's revelation, woe is me. No, I need fresh revelation for today because it's a new day.

> *So He came to Nazareth, where He had been brought up. And as His custom was, He went into the synagogue on the Sabbath day, and stood up to read. And He was handed the book of the prophet Isaiah. And when He had opened the book, He found the place where it was written: "The Spirit of the Lord is upon Me, because He has anointed Me to preach the gospel to the poor; He has sent Me to heal the brokenhearted, to proclaim liberty to the captives and recovery of sight to the blind, to set at liberty those who are oppressed; to proclaim the acceptable year of the Lord." Then He closed the book, and gave it back to the attendant and sat down. And the eyes of all who were in the synagogue were fixed on Him. And He began to*

say to them, "Today this Scripture is fulfilled in your hearing (Luke 4:16-21).

The Word teaches us that the works Jesus did we can do also (see John 14:12). The first time I read that I was intrigued and so began to study exactly what those "works" that Jesus did entailed. What I found in my studies was something I had never heard taught or preached before. As a matter of fact, true to our modern day culture of *instant* everything, I saw some fundamental truths completely ignored or overlooked because of the blindness inherent to those reared in this culture.

Let me name just a few of the foundational "works" Jesus did: He became of no reputation, divested Himself of deity, came to the earth and humbled Himself; He took on the form of a servant, and for the joy that was set before Him, He endured the cross. When He was despised, He did not reciprocate—just to name a few.

Those are the foundational "works" of Jesus. We jump immediately to the signs, wonders, and miracles, and wanting to emulate that aspect of His "works" without understanding the foundation that was laid in His life for those signs, wonders, and miracles to operate to the extent they did in His life.

Character—the Firm Foundation

Here is another key to the foundation lain in the life of Christ that few pay heed to: Jesus was raised in Nazareth. The name *Nazareth* means "separated, crowned, and sanctified."[3] For 30 years of His life, He was separated unto God; He was sanctified. He lived a separated life so He could be crowned with glory—30 years of the foundation of *character* to prepare Him for three and a half years of ministry. That is most of His life spent in preparation for 10 percent of His life spent in ministry. We want 30 years of ministry with only three years of preparation.

If we truly want to emulate Christ, and we truly want to "do the works" that He did, we need to reevaluate our concepts of exactly what is truly important to God from His perspective. It is not gifting, but character. Gifting is temporary—for this life, but character is eternal!

Now notice in verse 16 of Luke 4 that it was Jesus' custom to enter the Synagogue on the Sabbath day. Let me rephrase that: On the Seventh Day, Jesus' custom is to enter the temple.

We are the temple that Jesus is visiting on this Seventh Day! Do you comprehend this? Visitation is the norm on the Seventh Day according to the perspective of Heaven. Is it any wonder we are hearing countless numbers of testimonies from people all over the world who are having visitations from Jesus? Not only that, one of the most telling signs that you have been prepared by the Holy Spirit to have a visitation is the fact that the Lord birthed within you (He gave you that desire in your heart), a desire to know Him face to face! That is His calling card! Faithful is He who called, who also shall do it! (see 1 Thess. 5:24 KJV).

On this particular Sabbath day (Seventh Day), Jesus did something not recorded anywhere else: He stood up to read. Today, Jesus is arising within His people—the temple of our bodies. We are coming to the fullness of the stature of the knowledge of God on this Seventh Day! This is a picture of a son or daughter of God coming to maturity. It is the end of the age, and we will be prepared and ready for His return as we allow Him to fill us with His all in all.

He then began to read from the Book of Isaiah (vs. 18)— *"The Spirit of the Lord is Upon Me, because...."* You have the Holy Spirit within you because you have a purpose and a destiny to fulfill in this hour.

Continuing on with verse 18-19, *...because He has anointed Me to preach the gospel to the poor; He has sent Me to heal the brokenhearted, to proclaim liberty to the captives and recovery of sight to the blind, to set at liberty those who are oppressed; to proclaim the acceptable year of the Lord* (Luke 4:18-19).

God-Given Commission

This is your commission on this day. You have a calling, purpose, and destiny; and He gave you the tools you need to fulfill it! He sent the Holy Spirit to teach, comfort, equip, and enable each of us. Thank God that on this day, Jesus—the anointed One—will be arising within us to cause us to become all that we are called to be! The harvest *will* be reaped.

Now, look at this key: *Then He closed the book, and gave it back to the attendant and sat down. And the eyes of all who were in the synagogue were fixed on Him* (Luke 4:20).

On this Seventh Day, Jesus will take His rightful place upon the throne of our heart! It will be an act that will cause us to have our heart and our gaze fixed on Him. He will have our total attention as we finally come to the realization that He is all that truly matters; He is what our hearts have longed for.

In Luke 4:21, Jesus makes a statement that still resounds within my spirit: *"Today this scripture is fulfilled in your hearing."* If we have ears to hear what the Spirit of God is saying to this generation, we will see the fulfillment of what He is saying because we are hearing from Him! This is the day of the fulfillment of every covenant promise that has been released throughout God's Word! Can you hear the sound of Heaven for this generation? Can you hear the promise for you and your family? If you can, it will be fulfilled today!

ENDNOTES

1. Encarta Dictionary, s.v. necromancy

2. A.T. Robertson, "Chrysostom," *Word Pictures in the New Testament* (Nashville, TN: B&H Publishing Group).

3. Roswell Hitchcock, *Hitchcock's New and Complete Analysis of the Bible,* Wordsearch 8 software; http://www.wordsearchbible.com.

CHAPTER 10

Standing up in the Seventh Day

Jesus came into the synagogue on the Seventh Day, but on the Seventh Day He did something unique; He stood up. The Church of this hour is about to arise in a newness of life heretofore never seen. We are swiftly becoming the Church Triumphant, in action as well as in word!

I used to pray consistently, "Lord, less of me and more of you." If you study the life of Paul, he modeled a similar attitude. At the beginning of his ministry, it was a little of me and a little of You Lord. As he grew in relationship with the Lord and discovered his great lack and the Lord's abundant supply, his tone changed to less of me and more of You Lord. But by the end of his life we see a different picture as he communicated in words and action, Lord, all of you and none of me! I have since learned that a little bit is never enough! Our commitment to the Lord must be *all* of You Lord, and none of me! This is the picture we see repeatedly as we study the Scriptures concerning the Seventh Day. It is a day that will be given to total surrender to the Lord. It is a day of no compromise—of all or nothing. It is a day of divesting ourselves of every encumbrance and hindrance to become all that His Word says we are. It is a day of transformation!

All of you and none of me! You are the Body of Christ. It is the Seventh Day and Jesus is arising within us, and the Spirit of the Lord is upon us. That anointing is not just increasing incrementally, but it is about to explode within us as Jesus takes His rightful place in our hearts.

When Jesus was handed the Book in the synagogue, He stood up with all the strength and maturity of the Son of God and He spoke with authority. Then Jesus closed the Book and gave it back to the attendant, and He sat down. Now He is enthroned in your heart.

Making Him Feel at Home

When I was working at Trinity Broadcasting Network (TBN) many years ago, a friend came to visit me for a weekend from out of state. I said "Hey I've got to go to work, but make yourself at home."

Well, I got home that night and all the lights were off, so in an attempt to be polite, I tried to quietly sneak up to my room to go to bed. The problem was, I kept tripping over my furniture! I couldn't understand that, as I knew where the furniture was, or so I thought! In confusion and pain from hitting my shins, I turned on the light and discovered he had rearranged everything!

I woke him up and said, "What do you think you're doing?" He said, "You told me to make myself at home. I didn't like the way you decorated!"

And then it struck me: we do the same thing to Jesus. We say "Lord, come into my heart, and be the Lord of my life, but don't touch anything. And by the way, don't sit in my favorite chair."

As He releases your destiny to you on this Seventh Day and as He rises up within you, He will then sit upon the throne of your heart to rule and reign in your life and through your life.

Now it happened, as He went into the house of one of the rulers of the Pharisees to eat bread on the Sabbath, that they watched Him closely (Luke 14:1).

Spiritual Dropsy in the Church

Because of the hour of destiny that is upon us, and because of the love of the Father, even those steeped in a religious mind-set will be visited by the Lord on this Seventh Day. It is interesting to note, when it came to the Pharisees, the Scripture mentions quite frequently that Jesus visited them in their homes rather than the temple. I believe it was because the temple of their hearts had idols occupying the throne rather than the Lord.

And behold, there was a certain man before Him who had dropsy (Luke 14:2).

Dropsy was a condition where the individual would have water retention to such an extent that it imperiled life. The individual would become so bloated with liquid retention that it would suffocate the natural functioning of the other organs in the body and lead to death.

Most of the Church today has the condition of *spiritual* dropsy. We take the Word in repeatedly, going from meeting to meeting, conference to conference, and we do nothing with the Word. We seem to think that the quickest way to maturity in Christ is to gorge ourselves on a steady diet of conferences and meetings. We are deceived into thinking that quantity equates to maturity. The reality is that the quickest way to mature in Christ is to give away what you have! It is defined as seedtime and harvest in the Scriptures. If you want a greater anointing, give away what you have. Sow God's Word continually into the lives of others and into your own life, and you will begin to progress and increase in the Kingdom of God. We are not to hoard but to release.

Healing on the Sabbath

The Pharisees had been students of the Torah but had mixed the Word with worldly pursuits and ambitions. They believed that the traditions they had enacted, based on their *reason,* were on par with the Torah. *And Jesus spoke to the Pharisees, "Is it lawful to heal on the Sabbath?"* (Luke 14:3). Now Jesus, meeting the Pharisees where they lived so to speak, was testing their hearts and understanding of the Word. They were no longer testing Him. He was asking those who professed to be experts of the Word a basic question that anyone familiar with the Father's heart would have been able to answer; is it lawful to heal on the Sabbath? But they kept silent.

"And He took him and healed him, and let him go" (Luke 14:4). What did he do? Jesus modeled the truth of the heart of the Father and demonstrated the truth of God's Word. He healed the man! The Pharisees were unmoved, unrepentant, and missed the point.

I have often heard an expression that speaks volumes to this generation: The Lord often blesses what He does not inhabit. There is a time coming when an alleged revival will break out. There will be claims of miracles, signs and wonders, and boasts of the approval of God, not realizing the presence of God does not inhabit what they are embracing. This false revival will be exposed for the shallow counterfeit that it is.

Returning Revival to Body

When we first got saved, we always heard about revival meetings every summer. We were all told to "mark our calendars" and be sure to come out to these special times of the Lord's visitation. That wasn't revival. That was religious hype trying to equate

192

human attempts of reaching *for* God as God blessing His people with visitation. True revival is bringing something that was once alive back from the dead. Visitation from the Lord can encompass revival, but it is vastly more than that. It is an invasion of Heaven come to earth! It is the manifest presence of the living God inhabiting a geographic region to see His purposes fulfilled and to invest His essence into His people. It is a God-initiated encounter.

I believe the Lord is about to deal with our mind-sets of what revival truly is, rather than what we have always said it is, by visitation. We are about to experience the Lord to an extent that defies our ability to describe let alone understand. The manifest presence of God is beginning to be experienced in various regions and gatherings minutely. However, as we progress on in this Seventh Day, we will see regions and nations impacted and drastically changed by visitation. The Body of Christ will arise and become forerunners once again on the world stage. We will no longer be a byword to be mocked and ridiculed, but we will be a force that is recognized and as a force for good. As we begin to "hit our stride," the Church will be taken home, and those who remain will have had an example of what a "true Christian" is and will then be able to make an informed decision about whom they will serve. Even with this example, many will choose death rather than life, but God will have given a witness that will testify to His reality.

There will be a famine of the Word of God at the end of the age, especially when the Bride of Christ is taken home. Before that happens, we will know what true revival and awakening are. We are going to experience a visitation in the Church that will propel us to the uttermost parts of the earth to spread the good news of the Gospel to every tribe, tongue, and nation. The world will be awakened to the reality of God.

This visitation of the Lord will strengthen us with a resolve to reject the fear of humankind and a religious system devoid of power. The fear of humanity has been a snare that has kept many of the Lord's people in bondage far too long. Contrary to the traditions enacted by humankind, Bible college is not a prerequisite for preaching God's Word. If that were the case, none of us would be here! The disciples—uneducated and unlearned men—spent time in the presence of Him, who is Truth, and their influence changed history. None of them had a piece of paper with a nice seal on it. In the denominational world, there are rules about which college you have to attend. Humanity has injected himself into the process of ministry. The *real* prerequisite is to spend time with Jesus.

Let me make this disclaimer: I am *not* against going to Bible college and studying for the ministry. What I am saying is if we are to be truthful, Scripture does not *require* us to go to a manmade institution in order to be qualified to preach or teach the Word. I have spent countless hours both learning and teaching in Bible schools and seminaries around the world, and I have enjoyed every minute of it. I am not against higher education and study!

It is time for the people of God to arise and do what He has told us to do. In the process of being obedient to the great commission, if He tells you to go to Bible college, then go to Bible college.

Arise From Your Infirmities

*After this there was a feast of the Jews, and Jesus went up to Jerusalem. Now there is in Jerusalem by the Sheep **Gate** a pool, which is called in Hebrew, Bethesda, having five porches. In these lay a great multitude of sick people, blind, lame, paralyzed, waiting for the moving of the water. For an angel went down at a certain time into the pool and stirred up the water; then whoever stepped in first, after the stirring of* *the water, was made well of whatever disease he had. Now a certain man was there who had an infirmity thirty-eight years. When Jesus saw him lying there, and knew that he already had been **in that condition** a long time, He said to him, "Do you want to be made well?" The sick man answered Him, "Sir, I have no man to put me into the pool when the water is stirred up; but while I am coming, another steps down before me." Jesus said to him, "Rise, take up your bed and walk." And immediately the man was made well, took up his bed, and walked. And that day was the Sabbath* (John 5:1-9).

This Seventh Day Scripture has great significance, not only for the Body of Christ, but Israel also. On this Seventh Day, the Lord is going to miraculously visit His covenant people and they will arise from their bed of infirmity into fullness of life. As the Spirit of the Lord moves upon Israel, many will be touched and transformed before they realize that it was their Messiah who visited them. However, when they do realize who He is, they will follow Him joyfully.

We must be sensitive and focused on whatever the Spirit of God is doing right now. We must be lovers of the Word of God and lovers of the God of the Word. As we are in the Word and God begins to stir that Word up in our hearts, we must immediately respond so we may be released into present revelation.

The Season of Release

As I said in a previous chapter, I have been studying on translation by faith for about eight years now, and just recently the Lord gave me an amazing insight. I didn't even recognize it until about two months after the event. I was given a prophetic word by a brother in Ireland, written on a small slip of paper which he handed to me as I was entering the Church where we were ministering. After reading the note, I set it aside and forgot about it for two months. It was a couple of months later when I started fasting and studying the Word that I was reminded by the Lord about that note.

This is what was written on the note: Isaiah 58:12 *Those from among you Shall build the old waste places; you shall raise up the foundations of many generations; and you shall be called the Repairer of the Breach, The Restorer of Streets to Dwell In.*

Now, what has that got to do with translation by faith? The word *old* means "properly concealed vanishing point, time out of mind."[1] The Lord began to speak to my spirit and revealed to me that we have entered the season of release for these types of miracles. Just as we were once incapacitated and needing someone to "help us to the water," we are now being immersed in the waters of revelation which will bring healing or restoration to our spiritual senses. This will enable us to walk in paths formerly hidden to us, a place of *time out of mind*—a properly concealed vanishing point that will allow us to walk after the spirit and not after the flesh.

This generation shall reestablish these ancient paths for the children of God, and we will be whole!

"Jesus said to him, "Rise, take up your bed and walk! And immediately, the man was made well..." (John 5:8-9). It is the Seventh Day. We have to be aware of what our Father is doing through His Word. We have to respond to the stirring of the Water of the Word. For those who have not fine-tuned their ears to hear the voice of the Spirit, this may be a challenging season. We are being asked by the Lord on this day if we are willing to fulfill our destiny. Are we willing to obey the mandate of Heaven and yield to the reproof of the Father as He culls the world out of us and consecrates us to His purposes? To do so, we must be able to hear His voice and to respond to that voice in obedience.

*Now as **Jesus** passed by, He saw a man who was blind from birth. And His disciples asked Him, saying, "Rabbi, who sinned, this man or his parents, that he was born blind?" Jesus answered, "Neither this man nor his parents sinned, but that the works of God should be revealed in him. I must work the works of Him who sent Me while it is day; **the** night is coming when no one can work. As long as I am in the world, I am the light of the world." When He had said these things, He spat on the ground and made clay with the saliva; and He anointed the eyes of the blind man with the clay. And He said to him, "Go, wash in the pool of Siloam" (which is translated, Sent). So he went and washed, and came back seeing. Therefore the neighbors and those who previously had seen that he was blind said, "Is not this he who sat and begged?" Some said, "This is he." Others **said**, "He is like him." He said, "I am **he**." Therefore they said to him, "How were your eyes opened?" He answered and said, "A Man called Jesus made clay and anointed my eyes and said to me, 'Go to the pool of Siloam and wash.' So I went and washed, and I received sight." Then they said to him, "Where is He?" He said, "I do not know." They brought him who formerly was blind to the Pharisees. Now it was a Sabbath when Jesus made the clay and opened his eyes* (John 9:1-14).

The first lesson we learn from John chapter 9 is one we would do well to emulate in our own lives. When they saw the condition of the man who was born blind, rather than jump to a conclusion, they asked Jesus what the cause of this blindness was; that was wisdom. In other words, what is the root cause of this condition? Too often, believers are found putting bandages on symptoms rather than eradicating the disease by ascertaining the cause. When we do that, we often sow confusion as the symptoms many times return, and in an attempt to spiritualize or at the least, try and keep our super-spiritual facade intact, we point the finger of blame: "If you just had enough faith you would keep your healing."

A heart of humility will always rely upon the wisdom of God rather than fleshly presumption.

Once Jesus answered His disciple's question, He spit on the ground and made mud, put it on the man's eyes and told him to go wash in the pool of Siloam, which means sent. (See John 9:6-8.) Question: How many of us on a regular basis see into the realm of the Spirit? How many of us regularly meet with Jesus face to face? (I'm not spiritualizing this; I literally mean, do you *see* Him face to face?) If you do not, then when you were born again, you were born blind; you are spiritually blind!

> John 3:3 says, *Jesus answered and said to him, "Most assuredly, I say to you, unless one is born again, he cannot see the kingdom of God."*

Jesus said this in answer to Nicodemus who came to him at night and began to question him about the Kingdom of God. What Jesus said is staggering! He was telling Nicodemus that if you are born again, you can see the Kingdom of God! The qualifier is, are you born again? We have limited ourselves and adhered to man-made traditions and denominational doctrines that are contrary to Scripture. Whose word will you believe? God's Word or the word of man or woman?

The man born blind was released from his blindness when he obeyed Jesus' command: Go and wash in the pool of Siloam. Are we washing in the Water of His Word as 'sent ones' with a commission from the Lord to reach our generation for Christ? Are we yielding to the passion of our Lord's heart to release the Kingdom of Heaven on earth and to be lights to this dark and perverse generation? It is in obedience, as we continue to commune with our

Lord in His Word, that our eyes are opened and we begin to *see* with clarity and to *know* Him as a friend, face to face!

The works of God are about to be revealed in you and released through you. As a terminal generation, an end-time Bridal Company of Believers, we are called to take part in the "final act" in a 6,000-year drama. We have been positioned by the wisdom of God in this season as part of the final generation. We have purpose, and we have a destiny to fulfill early in the morning on this Seventh Day.

A trumpet blast is about to sound, and the words, *"It is finished!"* pronounced. But before it does, we will be transfigured and live and move and have our being *in Him*! We will dwell under the canopy of His glory, and we will release Heaven on earth. We will witness every covenant promise being fulfilled in this generation. We will be "complete in Him," and we will cease from our own works and enter into His rest.

This is the most propitious day in recorded history to be alive! And our heavenly Father chose *you* to see His will come to pass and to partake of the final victory!

There is a wealth of revelation being released to us on this Seventh Day. You have an extraordinary destiny in God. The Spirit of the Lord has been proclaiming, "This is *your* hour!" Jesus is raising us up to rule and reign with Him in this world. He is opening His Word, and He is releasing to this generation remarkable revelation and insight so the longing of our hearts will be fulfilled; we will know Him beyond reason!

> Father, I thank you so much for your Word. Lord, I thank you that we are an Enoch generation. Father, I pray again that You would release into Your people revelation knowledge—insight that they may hear Your heart's cry

in this hour and they will become everything You say they are. Lord, let them begin to walk in realms of revelation that cultivates within them an intimacy beyond anything they could ask or think. I thank You, according to Your Word, they are becoming the mature sons of the living God that all of creation has been longing to see come forth. This is our finest hour, and I thank You Lord for the incomprehensible privilege you have bestowed upon us that we may partake of this final great harvest and witness the conclusion of man's stewardship over this earth. In Jesus' name, Amen.

ENDNOTE

1. James Strong, *Strong's Concordance of the Bible* (Peabody, MA: Hendrickson Publishers, 1996) ref. 5769.

Promises of the Seventh Day

The number seven is a powerful number in Scripture:

It is the number of rest, covenant promise fulfilled, and completion. It is the symbol of spiritual perfection either of good or of evil.

- The Sabbath is the Seventh Day.

- Enoch, the seventh from Adam, "was not, for God took him" (Gen. 5:24).

- Moses was the seventh from Abraham.

- In Genesis 12:2-3 (KJV) is given the seven-fold blessing pronounced by God upon Abraham:

  1. "I will make of thee a great nation,"

  2. "I will bless thee,"

  3. "I will make thy name great,"

  4. "Thou shalt be a blessing,"

  5. "I will bless them that bless thee,"

  6. I will "curse him that curseth thee,"

7. "In thee shall all families of the earth be blessed."

- The people of Israel were given a sevenfold promise from God secured in its beginning and ending with the declaration, *"I am the Lord"* in Exodus 6:6-8 (KJV).

  1. "I will bring you out from under the burdens of the Egyptians,"

  2. "I will rid you out of their bondage,"

  3. "I will redeem you with a stretched-out arm and with great judgments,"

  4. "I will take you to me for a people"

  5. "I will be to you a God,"

  6. "I will bring you in unto the land concerning the which I did swear to give it to Abraham, to Isaac, and to Jacob,"

  7. "I will give it to you for an heritage."

- In Leviticus 14, where the law of the leper is stated, he was to be sprinkled seven times (Lev. 14:7).

- There were seven Feasts of Jehovah, some of which lasted for seven days.

- In Numbers 23:29 when Balak, the Moabite king, would have the hireling Balaam to curse Israel, he set up for him seven altars, and prepared seven bullocks and seven rams, the perfection of idolatrous worship.

- In Joshua 6, when the people of God encompassed Jericho, they were preceded by seven priests carrying seven trumpets of ram's horns, and on the Seventh Day, at God's command, encompassed it seven times.

- In the Book of Judges, seven weak things were used by God to confound the mighty, marking the spiritual perfection of God's works of deliverance.

  1. In Judges 3:21, He made use of a left-handed man.

  2. In Judges 3:31, He made use of an ox-goad.

  3. In Judges 4:4, He made use of a woman.

  4. In Judges 4:21, He made use of a tent-peg.

  5. In Judges 9:53, He made use of a piece of millstone.

  6. In Judges 7:20, He made use of pitchers and trumpets.

  7. In Judges 15:15, He made use of the jaw-bone of an ass.

- In First Samuel 16:10, are found the seven sons of Jesse.

- In Second Samuel 21:9, we find the seven sons of Saul.

- Matthew 12:45 refers to seven more wicked spirits—a picture of evil reaching the pinnacle of evil.

- In Matthew 18:22, the Lord Jesus Christ laid down the perfect measure of forgiveness—70 times 7.

- In Mark 16:9, Mary Magdalene is spoken of with this comment: "Out of whom He had cast seven demons," showing us the very climax of iniquity.

- In Acts 6:3, we read that the apostles instructed the disciples to choose seven men, "of honest report, full of the Holy Ghost and wisdom" (KJV).

- In Acts 13:19 is recorded how God, fighting in behalf of His people Israel, destroyed seven nations in the land of Canaan.

- Seven epistles were written to the churches and canonized, giving perfect instruction in all matters pertaining to life and godliness.

- Seven letters to the churches in the Revelation give insight into church history.

- Also, in Revelation we find seven candlesticks, seven stars, seven lamps, seven angels, and seven spirits, while seven seals secure the book completely, and in seven last plagues is "fulfilled the wrath of God" (see Rev. 15:1).

Here is another profound example of the number seven in Scripture:

Suppose you were asked to construct a genealogy of real people, but there are certain constraints. The number of words in this genealogy must:

- Be evenly divisible by seven (with no remainders)

- The number of letters must be divisible by seven

- The number of vowels and consonants must be divisible by seven

- The number of words that begin with a vowel must be divisible by seven

- The number of words that occur more than once must be divisible by seven

- The number of words that occur in more than one form must be divisible by seven

- The number of words that occur only in one form must be divisible by seven

- The number of names in the genealogy must be divisible by seven

- The number of male names must be divisible by seven

- The number of generations in the genealogy must be divisible by seven

This would seem to be next to impossible to do, yet that exactly describes the genealogy of Jesus as given in the Gospel of Matthew 1:2-17.

Seventh Day Scriptures (Sabbath Day)

Exodus 12:15-20 (KJV)

Seven days shall ye eat unleavened bread; even the first day ye shall put away leaven out of your houses: for whosoever eateth leavened bread from the first day until the seventh day, that soul shall be cut off from Israel. And in the first day there shall be an holy convocation, and in the seventh day there shall be an holy convocation to you; no manner of work shall be done in them, save that which every man must eat, that only may be done of you. And ye shall observe the feast of unleavened bread; for in this selfsame day have I brought your armies out of the land of Egypt: therefore shall ye observe this day in your generations by an ordinance for ever. In the first month, on the fourteenth day of the month at even, ye shall eat unleavened bread, until the one and twentieth day of the month at even. Seven days shall there be no leaven found in your houses: for whosoever eateth that which is leavened, even that soul shall be cut off from the congregation of Israel, whether he be a stranger, or born in the land. Ye shall eat nothing leavened; in all your habitations shall ye eat unleavened bread.

Exodus 13:6-7 (KJV)

Seven days thou shalt eat unleavened bread, and in the seventh day shall be a feast to the Lord. Unleavened bread shall be eaten seven days; and there shall no leavened bread be seen with thee, neither shall there be leaven seen with thee in all thy quarters.

Exodus 16:25-30 (KJV)

And Moses said, Eat that to day; for to day is a sabbath unto the Lord: to day ye shall not find it in the field. Six days ye shall gather it; but on the seventh day, which is the sabbath, in it there shall be none. And it came to pass, that there went out some of the people on the seventh day for to gather, and they found none. And the Lord said unto Moses, How long refuse ye to keep my commandments and my laws? See, for that the Lord hath given you the sabbath, therefore he giveth you on the sixth day the bread of two days; abide ye every man in his place, let no man go out of his place on the seventh day. So the people rested on the seventh day.

Exodus 20:8-11 (KJV)

Remember the sabbath day, to keep it holy. Six days shalt thou labour, and do all thy work: But the seventh day is the sabbath of the Lord thy God: in it thou shalt not do any work, thou, nor thy son, nor thy daughter, thy manservant, nor thy maidservant, nor thy cattle, nor thy stranger that is within thy gates: For in six days the Lord made heaven and earth, the sea, and all that in them is, and rested the seventh day: wherefore the Lord blessed the sabbath day, and hallowed it.

Exodus 23:12 (KJV)

Six days thou shalt do thy work, and on the seventh day thou shalt rest: that thine ox and thine ass may rest, and the son of thy handmaid, and the stranger, may be refreshed.

Exodus 24:16 (KJV)

And the glory of the Lord abode upon mount Sinai, and the cloud covered it six days: and the seventh day he called unto Moses out of the midst of the cloud.

Exodus 31:13-17 (KJV)

Speak thou also unto the children of Israel, saying, Verily my sabbaths ye shall keep: for it is a sign between me and you throughout your generations; that ye may know that I am the Lord that doth sanctify you. Ye shall keep the sabbath therefore; for it is holy unto you: every one that defileth it shall surely be put to death: for whosoever doeth any work therein, that soul shall be cut off from among his people. Six days may work be done; but in the seventh is the sabbath of rest, holy to the Lord: whosoever doeth any work in the sabbath day, he shall surely be put to death. Wherefore the children of Israel shall keep the sabbath, to observe the sabbath throughout their generations, for a perpetual covenant. It is a sign between me and the children of Israel for ever: for in six days the Lord made heaven and earth, and on the seventh day he rested, and was refreshed.

Exodus 34:21 (KJV)

Six days thou shalt work, but on the seventh day thou shalt rest: in earing time and in harvest thou shalt rest.

Exodus 35:2-3 (KJV)

Six days shall work be done, but on the seventh day there shall be to you an holy day, a sabbath of rest to the Lord: whosoever doeth work therein shall be put to death. Ye shall kindle no fire throughout your habitations upon the sabbath day.

Leviticus 23:3 (KJV)

Six days shall work be done: but the seventh day is the sabbath of rest, an holy convocation; ye shall do no work therein: it is the sabbath of the Lord in all your dwellings.

Leviticus 23:8 (KJV)

But ye shall offer an offering made by fire unto the Lord seven days: in the seventh day is an holy convocation: ye shall do no servile work therein.

Numbers 19:11-13 (KJV)

He that toucheth the dead body of any man shall be unclean seven days.

He shall purify himself with it on the third day, and on the seventh day he shall be clean: but if he purify not himself the third day, then the seventh day he shall not be clean. Whosoever toucheth the dead body of any man that is dead, and purifieth not himself, defileth the tabernacle of the Lord; and that soul shall be cut off from Israel: because the water of separation was not sprinkled upon him, he shall be unclean; his uncleanness is yet upon him."

Numbers 19:19-20 (KJV)

And the clean person shall sprinkle upon the unclean on the third day, and on the seventh day: and on the seventh day he shall purify himself, and wash his clothes, and bathe himself in water, and shall be clean at even. But the man that shall be unclean, and shall not purify himself, that soul shall be cut off from among the congregation, because he hath defiled the sanctuary of the Lord: the water of separation hath not been sprinkled upon him; he is unclean.

Numbers 28:25 (KJV)

And on the seventh day ye shall have an holy convocation; ye shall do no servile work.

Numbers 31:19-20 (KJV)

And do ye abide without the camp seven days: whosoever hath killed any person, and whosoever hath touched any slain, purify both yourselves and your captives on the third day, and on the seventh day.

And purify all your raiment, and all that is made of skins, and all work of goats' hair, and all things made of wood.

Numbers 31:20-24 (KJV)

And purify all your raiment, and all that is made of skins, and all work of goats' hair, and all things made of wood.

And Eleazar the priest said unto the men of war which went to the battle, This is the ordinance of the law which the Lord commanded Moses;

Only the gold, and the silver, the brass, the iron, the tin, and the lead,

Every thing that may abide the fire, ye shall make it go through the fire, and it shall be clean: nevertheless it shall be purified with the water of separation: and all that abideth not the fire ye shall make go through the water.

And ye shall wash your clothes on the seventh day, and ye shall be clean, and afterward ye shall come into the camp.

Deuteronomy 5:14-15 (KJV)

But the seventh day is the sabbath of the Lord thy God: in it thou shalt not do any work, thou, nor thy son, nor thy daughter, nor thy manservant, nor thy maidservant, nor thine ox, nor thine ass, nor any of thy cattle, nor thy stranger that is within thy gates; that thy manservant and thy maidservant may rest as well as thou.

And remember that thou wast a servant in the land of Egypt, and that the Lord thy God brought thee out thence through a mighty hand and by a stretched out arm: therefore the Lord thy God commanded thee to keep the sabbath day.

Deuteronomy 16:8 (KJV)

Six days thou shalt eat unleavened bread: and on the seventh day shall be a solemn assembly to the Lord thy God: thou shalt do no work therein.

Joshua 6:4 (KJV)

And seven priests shall bear before the ark seven trumpets of rams' horns: and the seventh day ye shall compass the city seven times, and the priests shall blow with the trumpets.

Joshua 6:15-16 (KJV)

And it came to pass on the seventh day, that they rose early about the dawning of the day, and compassed the city after the same manner seven times: only on that day they compassed the city seven times.

And it came to pass at the seventh time, when the priests blew with the trumpets, Joshua said unto the people, Shout; for the Lord hath given you the city.

Judges 14:15-20 (KJV)

And it came to pass on the seventh day, that they said unto Samson's wife, Entice thy husband, that he may declare unto us the riddle, lest we burn thee and thy father's house with fire: have ye called us to take that we have? is it not so? And Samson's wife wept before him, and said, Thou dost but hate me, and lovest me not: thou hast put forth a riddle unto the children of my people, and hast not told it me. And he said unto her, Behold, I have not told it my father nor my mother, and shall I tell it thee? And she wept before him the seven days, while their feast lasted: and it came to pass on the seventh day, that he told her, because she lay sore upon him: and she told the riddle to the children of her people. And the men of the city said unto him on the seventh day before the sun went down, What is sweeter than honey? And what is stronger than a lion? And he said unto them, If ye had not plowed with my heifer, ye had not found out my riddle. And the Spirit of the Lord came upon him, and he went down to Ashkelon, and slew thirty men of them, and took their spoil, and gave change of garments unto them which expounded the riddle. And his anger was kindled, and he went up to his father's house. But Samson's wife was given to his companion, whom he had used as his friend.

2 Samuel 12:15-23 (KJV)

And Nathan departed unto his house. And the Lord struck the child that Uriah's wife bare unto David, and it was very sick.

David therefore besought God for the child; and David fasted, and went in, and lay all night upon the earth.

And the elders of his house arose, and went to him, to raise him up from the earth: but he would not, neither did he eat bread with them.

And it came to pass on the seventh day, that the child died. And the servants of David feared to tell him that the child was dead: for they said, Behold, while the child was yet alive, we spake unto him, and he would not hearken unto our voice: how will he then vex himself, if we tell him that the child is dead?

But when David saw that his servants whispered, David perceived that the child was dead: therefore David said unto his servants, Is the child dead? And they said, He is dead.

Then David arose from the earth, and washed, and anointed himself, and changed his apparel, and came into the house of the Lord, and worshipped: then he came to his own house; and when he required, they set bread before him, and he did eat.

Then said his servants unto him, What thing is this that thou hast done? thou didst fast and weep for the child, while it was alive; but when the child was dead, thou didst rise and eat bread.

And he said, While the child was yet alive, I fasted and wept: for I said, Who can tell whether God will be gracious to me, that the child may live?

But now he is dead, wherefore should I fast? can I bring him back again? I shall go to him, but he shall not return to me.

1 Kings 20:29 (KJV)

And they pitched one over against the other seven days. And so it was, that in the seventh day the battle was joined: and the children of Israel slew of the Syrians an hundred thousand footmen in one day.

Esther 1:10-11 (KJV)

On the seventh day, when the heart of the king was merry with wine, he commanded Mehuman, Biztha, Harbona, Bigtha, and Abagtha, Zethar, and Carcas, the seven chamberlains that served in the presence of Ahasuerus the king, to bring Vashti the queen before the king with the crown royal, to shew the people and the princes her beauty: for she was fair to look on.

Ezekiel 30:19-26 (KJV)

Thus will I execute judgments in Egypt: and they shall know that I am the Lord.

And it came to pass in the eleventh year, in the first month, in the seventh day of the month, that the word of the Lord came unto me, saying,

Son of man, I have broken the arm of Pharaoh king of Egypt; and, lo, it shall not be bound up to be healed, to put a roller to bind it, to make it strong to hold the sword.

Therefore thus saith the Lord God; Behold, I am against Pharaoh king of Egypt, and will break his arms, the strong, and that which was broken; and I will cause the sword to fall out of his hand.

And I will scatter the Egyptians among the nations, and will disperse them through the countries.

And I will strengthen the arms of the king of Babylon, and put my sword in his hand: but I will break Pharaoh's arms, and he shall groan before him with the groanings of a deadly wounded man.

But I will strengthen the arms of the king of Babylon, and the arms of Pharaoh shall fall down; and they shall know that I am the Lord, when I shall put my sword into the hand of the king of Babylon, and he shall stretch it out upon the land of Egypt.

And I will scatter the Egyptians among the nations, and disperse them among the countries; and they shall know that I am the Lord.

Hebrews 4:4-10 (KJV)

For he spake in a certain place of the seventh day on this wise, And God did rest the seventh day from all his works.

And in this place again, If they shall enter into my rest.

Seeing therefore it remaineth that some must enter therein, and they to whom it was first preached entered not in because of unbelief:

Again, he limiteth a certain day, saying in David, To day, after so long a time; as it is said, To day if ye will hear his voice, harden not your hearts.

For if Jesus had given them rest, then would he not afterward have spoken of another day.

There remaineth therefore a rest to the people of God.

For he that is entered into his rest, he also hath ceased from his own works, as God did from his.

Study and Reference Material

Below is a partial list of materials I have used in my studies over the years. They should prove beneficial to the student of the Word that desires to delve deeper into the subject matter of this, or any other, book.

The Old Testament Pseudepigrapha Volume 1

The New Testament Pseudepigrapha Volume 2

Dake's Study Notes by Finis Dake

E.W. Bullinger's notes found in the Companion Bible

Number in Scripture by E.W. Bullinger

Symbols and Types by Kevin Conner

The JPS Guide to Jewish Traditions by Ronald Eisenberg

The Hebraic Roots Version Scriptures

Hitchcock's New and Complete Analysis of the Bible by Roswell Hitchcock

Vincent's Word Studies in the New Testament

Word Studies in the Greek New Testament by Kenneth S. Wuest

The Complete Word Study Dictionary—Old and New Testament

The Zondervan Pictorial Encyclopedia of the Bible Volumes 1-5

Theological Dictionary of the New Testament Volumes 1-10

The Complete Works of Josephus

The Works of Philo

The IVP Bible Background Commentary New Testament

Strong's Exhaustive Concordance

Vine's Expository Dictionary of Old and New Testament Words

Young's Analytical Concordance to the Bible

ABOUT THE AUTHOR

Throughout the years, many churches, cities, and nations have been touched and inspired by the life-changing power of God flowing through Bruce Allen.

Gifted in the prophetic and teaching ministry, the Lord uses Bruce to impart, activate, and release individuals and churches into deeper realms of the Spirit. A compelling presence of the Holy Spirit permeates the atmosphere, and it is not unusual for unique signs, wonders, and miracles to flow freely in each meeting.

The Father-heart of God is evidenced in Bruce's ministry as the presence and glory of the Lord is released, drawing many back to the Father and causing many to draw deeply from the well of His presence.

The mandate of Still Waters International is to "Prepare the way of the Lord and make straight paths for His feet." This mandate focuses not only on the soon return of the Lord, but also for those who have been hungering for the presence of God in a deeper way in their life.

Still Waters International Ministries
Address: PO Box 1001 Chewelah, WA 99109
Phone: 509-340-1369
E-mail: abidesinrest@msn.com
Web site: www.stillwatersinternational.org